'UnMarrying ... *it is truly like to experience a breakup or divorce. Maria shares her journey in a clever and thought provoking way. She is so relatable and answers the questions people are afraid to ask. She also offers loads of resources and made reading this subject a comfortable, hopeful and page-turning experience. You will feel clearer . . . as well as empowered with new possibilities. I highly recommend this book if the thought of breaking up or divorcing flutters through your mind more often than you would like.* —Kathy Greidanus, Cl. Hyp., Rapid Transformational Therapy Practitioner

Wow! As a guy who has been divorced (my ex left me), I can see so many similarities in my own end of times. Maria's storytelling has enabled me to empathize even more with my ex-wife and the tough choices she must have had. Her story tugs at the heartstrings knowing that many others struggle with these same tough decisions. I highly recommend 'UnMarrying My Best Friend' to those at an impasse in their relationship and to anyone else who is intrigued with a well-written, truly personal, human interest story. —Jack Petterson

Maria's book is an informative and heartfelt account of a very difficult topic. It is well written and full of helpful resources for the reader. Truly a unique and important read for anyone going through this type of challenging time and beyond. —Heather

UnMarrying my best friend

UnMarrying my best friend

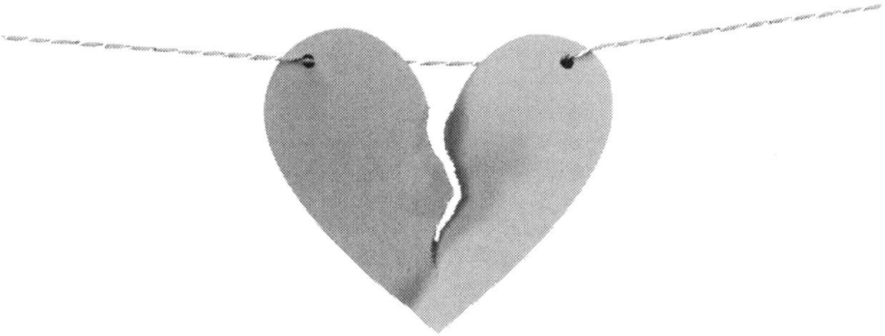

CHOOSING THE UNTHINKABLE

Divorcing after 32 years and tools that helped me survive the identity-slaying journey no one wants to talk about.

Maria Valentine

dimplesmedia

Published by Dimples Media, Mount Dora, Florida.

To our four children. You beat my heart and drive my soul.

Contents

Preface

This is a story of struggle as much as it's a story of hope and uncelebrated triumph. A story that begins with an ending and ends with a beginning.

I wrote this book two months after unmarrying my best friend of 35 years. Married for 32 years, college sweethearts for three, we were together and virtually inseparable for more years than we weren't. As a lifelong keeper of journals, I knew if I didn't commit to words on paper, this story of our uncoupling would disappear from my memory, blurring all reflection in a series of buried hurts.

No one really prepares us for the bitterness of our endings. Our world rolls on beginnings. First day of school. First day of summer. First kiss. First born. First house. Baptisms. Birthdays. Weddings.

We even celebrate our endings as new beginnings. Graduations, retirement parties and funerals send us off to new heights, greener pastures and a loving rebirth.

But divorce doesn't share that same glee. Riddled in shame, it's an ending with no greeting card category. At best, we paint our bitter endings with clever rationale. Bad yes. But we made it. We survived. We have lots to be grateful for. Memories to cherish. Laughter to remind. Everything happens for a reason. Timing's divine. You will survive.

When I began writing today, I didn't really know where my words would take me. I stood just outside the long shadow of heartbreak, in the dawn of a new life. Hopeful but still healing three years later.

But then, something just clicked.

I realized the meaning I attach to this bitter ending shapes my new beginning. I needed to reframe the meaning I've attached to this divorce or risk carrying its pain forward, polluting everyone around me and worse yet, my New Me.

So why not stroll past the bleak and lean into the bright? To new beginnings? To first light?

Uncelebrated and riddled in crushing shame, divorce has all the makings of keeping us in a cave. The victim. The victimized. Deals broken. Trust shaken. Dreams slayed. Hopes taken. It's got all the things that keep us down.

But we have a choice. To find the good inside the gore. To spin our tale with light not blight. To weave our meanings with love not fear. Shooting pains still surprise me now and then, but as long as I'm aware, I can let them move right through me.

I hope this look back of mine shows the uncomfortable and uncelebrated deserve our embrace. That even our bitter endings can be sweet beginnings.

This book is also for our four children. We all see our

family's unraveling differently. Just as their dad's look back is of a different colored thread than mine, so is each of our children's. It is my hope that someday if they read this, they will have a deeper understanding of my strand. If pieced all together, we can weave an even warmer blanket. That's the best of what a family can be. Acceptance and compassion all woven together. As the years march on, a family's weave takes on different colors and textures but it doesn't have to be unraveled forever. As long as we choose....

But more than anything I want our kids to know that the divorce has nothing to do with them. It was not done to them, for them or because of them. The health of their dad and I as a couple has as much to do with them as whether or not they like bacon or sausage. Ham or turkey. Chocolate or vanilla. That's right. Nothing to do with them.

It doesn't make us less of a family either. Marital status doesn't create or kill a family. We've all seen deeply connected families and deeply disconnected families, married or otherwise. It's our choice as a family, regardless of that status, to choose or not to choose, to make a new weave.

I've always believed that as parents, our number one job is to be the guardian of our children's hearts. We can't protect them from the harshness of life, but we can always be their safe place to land. A divorce doesn't have to change that.

I hold out my hand for those hearts their dad and I created. Our marital status will never change that.

Not a day passes when someone passes. Not a day begins

without an end in sight. Every second there are endings torturing the last man standing, unmercifully as if there were no tomorrow.

But there is a tomorrow. And that unmerciful, bitter pain of that ending you just felt? This too shall pass. You'll survive. Just like the countless endings you survived before.

This too shall pass.

In my darkest days, it was those four little words that kept floating back to me like a life preserver for my sinking ship. They became the salve for my battles and breakdowns. My breathing in. My breathing out.

This too shall pass.

It did and it still does.

Happiness is just as fleeting as heartbreak.

Accept. Detach. Surrender.

This book is a reflection of my biggest unraveling. The man I unmarried has been part of more of my beginnings than not, and with many more to come. Four beautiful children secure that future for him and me. Weddings, birthdays and celebrations to be.

Unmarrying my best friend may seem like an ending for us, but it's really a new beginning in a whole different weave.

Celebrate or not. It's ours to choose.

Names have been changed to protect identities.

Chapter I

Dear Mother-in-Law

I wrote this letter to my mother-in-law within a month of unmarrying. She had just learned of our divorce.

Dear Barbara,

I'm not sure how to express whatever it is I feel the need to express to you. For months, I've felt the need to write to you, as I believed it was the right thing to do. I have been part of your family for decades. A face in the tapestry of your life. If for no other reason than for recognition of the breakdown of that, I felt it necessary to tie a bow, and circle around the closure of all that.

Whatever that is, was and isn't any more.

Now, here I sit, dumbstruck and talking in circles, expressing that which I don't even know what. What do you say to a woman with whom you owe so much gratitude for raising a son with whom you will love 'til death, but now need to part? And, for a bundle of reasons that don't matter to anyone but he and I?

It is what it is.

Change. Growth. Life.

It's just hard. All of this is hard.

But that doesn't take away from whence he came. From a loving family and a mother who formed a man I will forever love.

So I guess what I want to really say is thank you. Thank you for being the You that is part of the man that I will love for the rest of my days. He and I may not be together the way we have been, but he will always be a part of me.

With love and so much gratitude,
Maria

I never received a response from my mother-in-law from this letter, nor did I ever speak to her again. Although hopeful for some sort of acknowledgement of our marriage ending, I wasn't surprised it didn't happen. A complicated relationship, hers and mine.

She passed away two years later.

Chapter 2

I Told Him I Couldn't be Faithful

I told him we needed to talk. It was Sunday morning. We usually sat on the front porch on weekend mornings, having our coffee, and strategizing the day ahead of us. No cause for alarm.

Or was there?

I knew I had to tell him. I just didn't know how or what to say.

I started anyway.

Coffee poured and all situated on our old matching rockers, small talk aside, I dove right in.

When I'm ready, I can't wait. I jump.

And jump I did.

Minutes before I walked out onto the porch, I remembered a billboard I had seen advertising a $99 divorce. That seemed like a good idea. Why couldn't we just do that?

So I popped the question.

Suffice it to say, years of struggle in this 32 year marriage had built up a rising emotional debt that put our relationship into bankruptcy. I couldn't pay off the debit all by myself. I had separated from him in the house nine months before thinking that would help. It didn't....

I had to make a choice. Accept the rising debt or push for payment.

I decided to forge ahead.

The day before, I walked endlessly around town channeling my best Forrest Gump hoping for answers. After hours of tears and bewilderment, a strange knowing inside broke through my box of limiting beliefs. Suddenly possibilities I had never considered before begged me for logical answers.

Outside my mental limitations, I fielded unheard of questions that gradually began opening my mind. I finally felt a tiny breeze of hope. A concept that had long escaped my lexicon.

Startled by this new found surge of what if's and maybe, I smiled. Cautiously. Knowing it too would pass.

Looking back on my Instagram feed, I see the post inspired by that moment. Our strength is as fleeting as our fears, I wrote. This too shall pass.

And it did. But it stayed around long enough for me to face this first jump off the high dive of divorce.

I knew if I made this jump, I could never go back. I could never go back to the land of Fix It And Hold My Breath. I couldn't pretend anymore. I couldn't act as if everything would be ok—-denying the truth that lay before me.

That's when I knew I would never be able to be faithful to him.

On every level. Literally and figuratively.

The life I wanted with him, and even felt at times, was constantly interrupted, dragging us both into the gutter.

I couldn't pretend and push it aside.

He showed me over and over that he was never going to join me in bringing our marriage to the level of fulfillment that I craved.

Try as we might, and for years, we just couldn't see eye to eye.

Mismatched goals. Disonnnected dreams.

Confusingly we had so many good times, sandwiched between seemingly endless bad times. Sparing for hours and days on end, with no resolution but to simply wear out and walk on by, until the next go 'round brought this mighty virus back to life.

I knew that if I stayed in this Wait And See world any longer, I would be setting myself up for years of more of the same. Nothing was going to change. I was a happy person wrapped in an armor of fear. Fearing the realization that the only way Happy Maria could come to life was to cause a whole lot of pain for others.

Worse, I knew that if I did nothing, the unHappy Maria that remained was even more painful for others.

So I picked the lesser of two horror shows.

Wanting neither. But knowing I had to choose.

This is where my story begins.

This isn't a story about what brought all this on. A bashing or a tell-all. Or a story to rationalize anything. The work we did or didn't do. The things we did or didn't do. The promises we made and broke.

This is a story of how Something Just Clicked. That undeniable pure knowing that finally drives us past the brink. The works behind an impossible choice, and where it all lead.

Hopefully along the way, some a-ha moments will pop out to show how rolling the dice on yourself wins every time.

That Sunday morning I was on a precipice of massive growth and didn't know it. But one thing I did know was that you can only live in misalignment for so long before it starts wrecking havoc with your mind, body and soul.

Our values and beliefs colliding with our actions. Recipe for disaster.

I decided I couldn't live that way anymore. I couldn't act "as if" all was fine. It wasn't fine.

I had to leave Pretendyland.

I had no idea how. Let alone even believe that I had the courage to do so. At that moment, the idea of D-I-V-O-R-C-E seemed so far out and unspeakable to me.

I couldn't even say the word.

But I started anyway.

I jumped.

So I was thinking . . .

I can't be faithful to you.

I don't see any hope.

I'm unfulfilled and worn out.

How about we get one of those $99 divorces I see on the billboards?

As you might have guessed, this didn't go over well.

Not even close.

We stood on two different continents. Presenting any form of change was caustic at best.

It played out as horrifically as all our go 'rounds.

My reasoning that I would be a much better, stronger person, able to help him and our family better if I was free of the drama of our marriage was not appreciated in the least.

A blur of more sparring finally ended in something of a compromise.

Let's just sell this house.

Financial issues plagued us for decades and took a serious toll on both of us. Certainly it seemed, releasing the albatross of a first and second mortgage would help....

And so we sat with that. For the next week or so. We had to have something to hang onto when we departed on a dreamy

Caribbean cruise that our kids gave us for Christmas months before. A gift I wept in receiving because the kids knew better than he what our marriage really needed.

If only he had given that gift to me . . .

The era of Heartbreak & Disappointment begins.

Chapter 3

Pretendyland and Happiness is a Choice

I don't think there has ever been a more damaging belief than Happiness is a Choice when it comes to marriage. I was trapped in this riddle for decades, buying into the sunshine that I create my own happiness. That you can't look to others for your happiness, etc.

Well, I'm telling you right here, that's bullshizzle in a marriage.

I figured this out the day I separated from my husband.

Along the way to heal our marriage, I decided I needed to step away from it. The tension inside our relationship had become unbearable. I consider myself pretty hardy, but when it comes to bad vibes in my own bedroom, a place I consider my ultimate sanctuary, I get a little territorial.

I couldn't spare to share my place of peace with any bad vibes. Either the bad vibes would have to leave, or I would have to gather up my blankie and find a new place of peace.

Considering the situation, I didn't even ask him to leave. I just moved into the basement. Thankfully, we have a big enough house where I could test the waters on this preliminary peek off the high dive.

What happened surprised me.

The whirling dervish that moved me out of our bedroom came with no premeditation. This was my very first inspired action in many to come. One that took me over, no questions asked, with unstoppable power and courage. There was no getting around this move of complete and unsettling clarity.

I was firm and resolute, but still hopeful and expecting. Expecting that this would solve everything. That he would see what was playing out, (which in no way was a stunt), and lean in to try to hear me. And maybe even move past his anger and roll up his sleeves and work with me rather than against me.

But he didn't. He walked on by. And held firmly to his belief that this single move destroyed our marriage.

I'm finally realizing he was right.

It did.

It showed me that first waking morning that my happiness was actually tied to his. Away from the heaviness that blanketed our bedroom, behind a closed door in a twin bed in the basement, I awoke with an unfamiliar lightness. A lightness that would continue to reveal itself time and time again over the next 18 months.

Away from him, dare I thought, I felt . . . .hApPy.

So maybe destroy is a dramatic take on my move. Let's just say it precipitated it. It showed me that there was lightness beyond.

Kinda like how knowledge is power. Something like that.

And that's when it dawned on me what all of that two becomes one stuff is. You know in a marriage ceremony when you join your candle with his candle to create the flame of one?

I finally realized what that really meant. I finally realized that my happiness is actually all boogered-up in his.

If he's happy. . . I'm happy.

If he's unhappy . . . I'm unhappy.

If he's living in fear . . . I'm living in fear.

Etc. And likewise.

That's the part where marriage becomes work. We have to meet in the middle and recognize where each of us are at, and work together lest we become totally infected by the funk of the other.

Obviously that wasn't happening for us. Intermittently yes, but overall no.

But there was no denying for me that the funk was everywhere. All over the house. And most palpable in our bedroom. But at least I was downwind of it in the basement so it was diffused enough for me to feel an interesting new lightness.

I took note and held on.

It was at that point I knew there was no turning back to what was. I just didn't know what that meant, and was still in complete denial and utter terror that it was fatal. We lived in Pretendyland for so many years. Trying to put our best face on a relationship that had become so disconnected. You become so locked into a system on so many levels you can't imagine yourself living any differently. And after decades, your identity becomes so blurred with your relationship, family, community and career that change seems not only foreign, but impossible.

Pretendyland starts early and in earnest for most married mere mortals. We buy into the Hallmark movie and fall into the cancerous entitlement of 'Til Death Do Us Part before the wedding thank you cards hit the mail. (Yes, real thank you cards are still a must even in this internet world. Don't get me started....)

Life piles on. Complacency takes root. And ultimately, compassion takes a back seat. Without compassion you have no connection. And without connection, you have no marriage.

You're roommates at best.

Frenemies at worst.

In our case, we were rivals in expectations. I expected more.

Welcome to Pretendyland.

Chapter 4

Married to a Married Man

It's been a year since that I told my husband I couldn't stay with him any longer. That morning on the front porch, broaching the unthinkable took me over like a storm out of nowhere. I knew exactly what I needed to do and had just enough courage to dare through it.

But now a year later, in the calm of time passed, I stumble in a fog searching for the words to simplify the why to our demise.

Even as I write this, I dodge around that icky word that starts with a D.

Because of Shame and Guilt.

Shame in failing and Guilt in choosing.

Shame and Guilt have their way with us whether we realize it or not. They sneak around messing with us, pushing us away from facing our deepest truths. And being who we really are meant to be.

My purpose in writing this book was primarily for reflection—for me and hopefully for my kids—to some day come to understand what happened to our family. At least from my point of view.

Certainly stringing together a few words to explain what happened can't be that hard. But it just is. The why to our demise was more than unmet needs and snarling standoffs.

In this journey of unmarrying, I have become keenly aware and respectful of my first morning thoughts. I've realized these first morning thoughts are closest to who I really am. And who I want to become.

Directly connected to my soul and free from the madness and confusion that short circuits us in the light of day, these thoughts show up as a whisper even as my eyes sleep tight.

They are my most trusted allies and teachers. My Buddha. My Yoda. My God.

Yielding to their wisdom, their guidance steadies me.

And a year ago, lead me to Here's why. . . .

I awoke that day to first light whispers pointing clearly to a realization that my husband and I shared entirely different views on life. Like a compass on steriods, I knew exactly where I needed to head.

We were best friends. We loved each other dearly and still do. (WAIT. I can't speak for him.) We raised four wonderful souls and created as close to a Hallmark movie as we could, but that just wasn't working for me anymore.

I was waking up too many mornings with thoughts that massively conflicted with my daily walk.

What I wanted more than anything was to live a lifestyle with a man who walked with me hand-in-hand, not fist to fist.

The continuous persuading and cheerleading in hopes that my husband would authentically join me, and not only have my back, but enthusiastically embrace a shared adventure, became so clearly hopeless with each passing day.

I knew what I needed to do that morning as I walked onto the porch. I didn't know exactly what words would form, but I knew it was time for them to come out.

That doesn't mean I didn't wince and cringe my way to the rockers.

Just like I didn't hold my breath a little bit before I started writing this chapter....

When raising our kids, one of the major guiding principles I tried to imbue in them was that every action we take originates from either a place of love or fear. I can't think of a single action in our human experience that can't be chiseled down to anything but.

When you whittle through any drama or dream in your life, I promise you'll find either a gremlin (fear) or a unicorn (love) staring back at you. Blooming from them will be all sorts of lack and scarcity (fear). Or abundance and possibility (love).

They say you find your yin for your yang, but at some point you may realize the pieces don't fit the way they used to fit. I crave a world of sunshine and unicorns, hearts and smiley faces, dreams and love. That just can't exist in the gremlin's world of toil and trouble, brooding and avoidance, limits and fear.

Try as I might to embrace my inner unicorn, before long my own gremlin would take over putting us right back in that familiar negative feedback loop. And 'round and 'round we'd go. Our gremlins just couldn't stop dancing to the same bitter tune, tearing up the place.

I saw my husband trapped in a mindset of fear. Married to his gremlin. I couldn't break that bond no matter how hard I tried. He was completely unavailable to me.

We all walk with our own gremlins and unicorns inside, but it's usually one or the other that predominantly calls the shots in our lives. Unfortunately the mighty gremlin guided my husband's actions all too often. And it was just too powerful for my sparkly unicorn to contend.

There was no way I could break that solid pairing.

I wanted more than he was willing to give. The longer I stayed the more unworthy I felt.

If I truly was the abundant thinker, powered by love and faith, why would I keep lowering my standards just because he wasn't buying what I was selling?

Because I was scared, confused and diminished.

But not anymore. Something just clicked.

Chapter 5

What I Miss

I remember shortly after our wedding, a friend asked me what I liked most about being married. I said sleeping with my husband. Really sleeping. The closeness. The connection. The pretzel-like entwining from limb to limb, lining up our heartbeats as we lowered the shades on another day.

He and I were really close. On every level. We were the couple that walked hand in hand (almost) until the day I moved out. We habitually reached for one another's hand whenever we walked anywhere. Hardware store or hot date. There was a closeness we shared that, even in our discourse, never went away. Rarely though, there were times when the tension was just way too steep and releasing our grip served the perfect punctuation for our madness.

Walking beside him without his hand in mine was awkward, uncomfortable and even a little unsettling when I noticed he hadn't grabbed for my hand.

Sleeping together was another one of those things. Although in times of trouble, and as the troubles piled on and escalated, sleeping together was the first thing that dropped away. Which was probably the canary in the coal mine.

Where you sleep is the most sacred place for anyone. It's where we're most vulnerable. It's where we let our guard down. Let go of today and refuel for tomorrow. It's serious business this bed we make.

I couldn't share vulnerable me in a space of no peace.

So I would send him away for the night, or I would leave for the night, to the point where I moved into another bedroom, then ultimately out of the house.

But up until then, I had gotten into the habit every night of hollering "Skin!" as I walked up the stairs. All the kids knew what this meant and would shout out to Dad that it was time to go to bed.

Going to bed at the same time, sleeping together, holding hands and the closeness we shared was the biggest thing that kept me tied to a relationship nearing its expiration date. The comfort of this touch, skin to skin, in our complicated life, was one thing that made me feel safe in a marriage that was often dangerously on the brink.

It's been said that in a relationship, a woman needs to feel seen, safe and understood. In the last few years of our marriage I felt all of those intermittently, but painfully inconsistently. The deficits were becoming too costly for me.

Something had to give.

But that doesn't mean I don't miss and long for the things that worked. Adding to the confusion is that the things that actually did work could never outweigh the things that didn't work.

In the timeliness of life, after I had already filed for divorce, I stumbled on a very telling-for-me book, hindsight as it were. I found it when I was searching for a different book about whether you should stay or go in a relationship. This caught my attention. What if I had made a mistake? I could always dismiss the final hearing....

I opened the book with caution....

I had read a few articles in the early days of our ending, double checking my sanity, but mostly, I followed my gut. Waking whispers have been my go-to in all of this.

But this book would've really saved a lot of second guessing.

One of the biggest takeaways I got from the book, *Too Good to Leave, Too Bad to Stay* by Mira Kirshenbaum is that you can't pro and con your way in or out of a relationship. There are simply deal breakers, regardless of all the pros that line up on the left side of the paper. Like in real estate, it's all about location, location, location. You might find the most gorgeous house for sale, with perfect layout, decor and lakeview, but if it's located next to a sewage treatment plant, that could be the deal breaker for you.

Same with relationships. It doesn't matter how much good there is if there's even just one mighty, deal breaking bad.

Our marriage was filled with many good things and I'll miss them all. Good that didn't go unnoticed and will never be forgotten. Like finding my freshly laundered underwear lined up and formed into a giant heart on our bed. Or being surprised with flowers from our garden in a vase on my desk. Or him telling me I'm beautiful a hundred times a day. "I can't help it. It just comes out," he would always say.

And our long walks. And long talks. And his silly. His funny. The way he made me laugh.

He and I couldn't have gone the distance of 35 years together, raising four kids with all the chaos of that, without having a pretty populated left side of the column. Or maybe it's because the deal breaker changed...or a new one was created.

None of these things, combined with the countless other good things we shared, held the weight of the handful of heavy things on the other side of the column. Things that, now, kids raised and out of the nest, couldn't be overlooked.

Something just had to give. And sadly it was us.

What I find surprising about this whole process of uncoupling has been how unclear it is. Just as marriage isn't like the movies, the ending of marriage isn't like the movies either.

It isn't as if one day you wake up and get a divorce and that's that.

No matter if you have kids or not. Relationships linger. We still help each other out.

I still bring him coffee. He still makes me laugh.

Even with the prevailing strain and awkwardness we now share two months after unmarrying. . . .

Chapter 6

The Icky Word

Even in our bitterest of battles I couldn't say it.

I'd say: I'm leaving. I can't take this anymore. I won't take this anymore. I'm done. But I could never say the D word.

When we got to talking more calmly about our situation, I'd dodge it as well. I'd call it splitting up, separating, or invent a new word like unmarrying . . . .

That day on the front porch when I told him my idea, the closest I got to saying the word was referencing a billboard for a $99 divorce.

After hearing me out, he immediately pushed the envelope and angrily said, "Are you saying you want a divorce?!!"

Gut punch. He had me against the ropes. I had a choice right then to plea uncle and go back to status quo. Or, brave my biggest fear.

"Yes," I said, dying inside knowing that I couldn't take it back.

Even if I could, I couldn't.

I had just released a truth that I had kept locked inside for . . . a very long time. . . .

To this day, almost two months post final hearing, I still can't say the word without dying a little more inside.

Why is that?

Let's explore. . . .

It's because of beliefs. And identity.

It's all connotative. How I feeeeeel about the word. What it says to me. About me. What I believe IS me.

The, who-do-I-think-I am part.

It hollers back loud and clear. That I'm a failure. That I blew it. That I gave up. That I'm weak. That I'm wrong. That I'm less than. . . .

All that icky, shaming, ego stuff. That gremlin-speak in our head that keeps us fighting, yet derails us at the same time.

It's totally one-sided. Irrational. False logic in the clearest sense. Like the difference between hearing that a stranger's car has been stolen, versus your own. The former is viewed through a lens of rationality and logic, sympathy and even empathy. But when it comes to your own car being stolen, that's a whole 'nother nightmare. Now it's personal and identity thwarting. A piece of who you (think you) are is stripped away.[1]

If I hear of a friend getting divorced, I feel massive empathy and likewise show compassion. It wouldn't cross my mind that my friend were anything but managing an impossible life situation.

But when it's me getting, and being divorced, that's so not right.

Considering how our beliefs shape us, it's probably a good time for me to start looking at my belief of who-do-I-really-think I am, and why I would believe this trashy self-talk.

That's when I start peeling back the onion. . . .

I grew up in a household where I never saw my parents fight or even argue. It wasn't until way later in life, in my thirties, when my mom began opening up to me about challenges in her own marriage.

And those were definitely challenges I could relate to,

---

1. The concepts in this chapter are mostly gleaned from The New Earth, by Eckhart Tolle. I don't know what I would have done without Tolle's teachings throughout this journey. The New Earth, is a must-have, must-read, highlight, dog-ear and re-read again and again book for any mere mortal with The Human Condition.

   Also significant to me during this time has been Dr. Brené Brown's book, Daring Greatly. Her lifelong research on vulnerability has been both fascinating and life changing for me.

which is an interesting part of this. . . . The whole, we marry a version of our father bit, but that's another story. . . .

So even knowing these challenges my mom faced with my dad, I always knew they were a pair, and 'til death would they part. I never could imagine anything but. Growing up to only see this ideal, I knew that's what I wanted. Without a doubt.

I believed that's the way it should be.

Kind of like how you solidly believe in the Hallmark Christmas movies, then look at your own tangled mess of a holiday and feel overwhelmed and defeated inside.

And how you suddenly realize that your facebook page truly screams FAKEbook. That every post you've ever done, even if believed to have been authentically posted in the joy of the moment, didn't tell the other side of the story. The side that didn't align with the face that you lead with and the walk you've talked.

Because nobody wants to see or hear that other side of that story. You think.

That's when you realize it isn't really FAKEbook as much as it's FEARbook. Authenticity is a scary place. It takes more courage to BE brave than to put on a brave face.

Vulnerability is more than skin deep.

When digging deeper, underneath that face, I started to clearly see what I was NOT.

I am not my circumstances, my life situation, my address, my business, my car or even my marital status.

Walking the walk of what we are NOT creates for us the

garbled mixed up life that causes all our suffering. Boldfaced misalignment.

We come into this world as a force of life, planted into a naked and wiggly little form of a body. As time passes, that form grows along with our clever little minds, creating all sorts of other forms, while indulging in the idea that all this stuff on the outside is really ME.

Then one day, if you're lucky, you get knocked off your feet, snap out of it, and realize none of the ornaments you've added to your tree is really the tree of life that resides inside.

This is where it gets even more airy fairy,

In my journey of being knocked off my feet, I've kept my struggle close to my vest, not telling even my closest friends or family. It's been a very solitary journey of crawling inside, reflecting, agonizing, judging and ultimately accepting. I've been forced to accept that you truly can't take it with you. That this isn't a race to the cake topper at our 50th anniversary party. Or that we are defined by the labels we place on ourselves and others. I may have a name, but that's not who I AM.

But even now, I still wrestle with this word Divorce. When I see it as a checkbox on a document, or when I'm having to reference the man I've called my husband for 32 years. . . . A simple mention of My Ex would suffice. But I continue to dodge that one too.

My struggle isn't in comprehending reality, but in reminding myself that my marital status doesn't define the ME that resides inside. The ME that upon death will exit the building, leaving behind all the forms and fun that I created while riding on this beautiful bouncy ball called Earth.

And in time I will become desensitized as I muscle through these pesky little moments where I'm faced to yet again remember not who I am, but who I am NOT.

That my name is Maria. And I was born into this body. And I got married. Then eventually got divorced.

But that none of these labels ARE me.

Tricky stuff.

Chapter 7

The Math Problem

Risk / Reward

I've never been good at statistics. In college it beat me up. Statistically, I was outnumbered by math; too many possibilities. I don't like to say I'm bad at math, because that's a dangerous self-fulfilling prophecy. If I'm not good to math, math won't be good to me. I respect math, and all it does, silently behind the scenes while no one is paying attention. Even if it confounds me.

And stats did that and more. Try as I might, I had the hardest time wrapping my head around the basics. What with all those variables and all that probability; like how to calculate all the different license plates possibilities, considering six characters of ten digits and 26 letters.

I made it through the class, by the grace of unicorns and rainbows, even getting a B, I think. But since then, everything to me boils down to one in a million. If I'm taking a chance, whether it's on a church raffle, a lottery ticket, or entering a coloring contest, it all feels the same. The odds are never in my favor. I've only got a one in a million chance in winning.

As the years piled on, and my marriage was getting more and more challenging, I realized I had to make a choice. I've talked about how I finally pulled the trigger and launched the D word, but how I actually decided which door to pick wasn't straight forward at all.

Until it was.

That's where math comes in and clears up everything. Whether you think you're good at math or not. Just respect it. It's always in the shadows.

A million times on the internet I've come across the quote (attributed to Einstein most often) that doing the same thing over and over again and expecting different results is insanity.

That started to sound a lot like my stats class. As in what's the probability of success? I was having an Einstein moment. I realized that I kept looking at my marriage the same way over and over again. I saw the problem, but I would convince myself that it wasn't that bad. It could be worse. We have so much good together. Our family. Our history. Our lifestyle. Our house. Etc.

So again and again, I would come up with one great idea after another to try to fix Us. Each plan would attempt to address our issues in practical, bite-sized, clearly defined and manageable ways. I'd get buy-in from him, and armed with a new plan, I would ramp up expectations.

All with the same result. Every time.

Expectations dashed.

So many possibilities. If only he would stick with our plan, I know we can get through this, I would always think. Each new plan started with hopeful first attempts that kept me interested, only to be followed by a predictable amnesia that we even had a plan. It was like we decided to train for a marathon, but his first wholehearted 5 am run with me was followed by oversleeping the next day, broken shoelaces the next, and ultimately not showing up the next.

Over and over and over and over again, and I'd get the same results.

Idea. Agreement. Hope. Hope dashed. Battle.

Repeat.

When I accepted that my attempts were truly never going to yield different results, I was able to look at the whole problem differently and take some advice from a quantifiable silent sage.

Math was waking me up.

Age may be just a number, but it's math and it's real. I literally wasn't getting any younger.

I realized with ever growing intensity that my age was advancing. Statistically, I likely only had about 20-30 years of active living ahead of me. When comparing that to the twenty seconds it took to span three decades of marriage, I took this math seriously.

I started to see the big picture when I was looking at the little picture.

I realized that I can blow through hours like a drunken sailor and by noon only have accomplished a few clever comments or shares on whatever social media grabbed my attention. And all with little fulfillment. Hours wasted away at the expense of all the good things I set out to do on that glorious new day.

If I could blow hours that unconsciously, certainly I must be blowing through years of my life just as unconsciously.

Like I had time to kill.

Then I woke up. Came to. And regained my consciousness.

Before that, I would find myself saying out loud, “Is this it? Is this all there is?”

I had gotten married, we raised four kids, got the house and a decent lifestyle to go along with it. It wasn’t perfect, but I seemed to be checking off all the boxes.

But it just wasn’t right. Our marriage wasn’t growing. It wasn’t getting any better. It was actually getting worse.

I started to feel like I was dying on the vine.

My last turn on this earth was being wasted away as I tried over and over and over again to create a fulfilling life with someone who just wasn’t ready for the harvest. Even the harvest takes a lot of work. But if you don’t do the work, you don’t get to reap what you worked so hard to sow.

We sowed and sowed and sowed together for years. Raising kids and navigating the storms of life together, and pretty successfully. We were looking at a beautiful crop, ready to harvest; to enjoy the fruits of our labor.

But we both needed to have our hands on one side of the basket. I could only gather so many fruits in my apron. Certainly not enough to satisfy my hunger.

That's when my special little daily disciplines started to make some sense to me.

Always on a quest to the new and improved me, I'm a big believer in daily routines to create healthy habits. I've kept a journal for most of my life, starting with a padlocked Holly Hobbie diary when I was in fourth grade. I just wasn't a very dedicated writer back then. I've always believed in the value of the free-flow expression in journal writing, but I was just too inconsistent at it to really experience the life changing benefits from it.

Until about 2000 days ago.

As of today, I started journal entry number 2,081. When I started, my goal was to journal every day for 30 days. I figured if I numbered each entry, I would be less likely to quit. My gremlins would have a field day with me. If I had gotten 17 days out, I'd be unmercifully chastised by a chorus of gremlins for going that far to just quit.

Thirty days came and went. A habit was formed. As the number grew and grew there was no way I could break the streak.

I had no grand plan for my journal, let alone any intention to re-read any of my drivel. But I bought into the idea that vomiting out my pain in private always has some silver lining. I added an additional requirement though. It couldn't be just a platform for pain. I had to write one thing I was grateful for every day.

That little rule has rewired my brain to consistently err on the side of positive, no matter the challenges I face. My entries are not all about my pain. When there's pain, absolutely, it's expressed, but when finishing up with a contagion of gratitude, my pain doesn't stand a strong chance of surviving too long.

So that's how I've been able to surf the storms of my struggles. But it's the math part that gave me the answer.

I "write" my journal audibly on my phone. There are a lot of journaling apps out there, but the one I chose and love is Day One. As I got used to the app, I realized I could tag entries. This is a great feature for whenever you want to go back and read an entry about a certain person, trip or holiday that you wrote about in the past. It makes the search so much easier.

At Day 565 I got the idea to tag one of my entries as a "fight" with my husband. I had always written about our battles in my journal, and it really had helped me gain deeper perspective in reflection. But now, moving forward, I thought that I should start quantifying how often these battles were actually happening, because it was feeling like a lot.

That's the sneaky thing about marriage. These standoffs become so blurred with our every day. Crafty denial obscures the bad days behind the good days.

Because if we only knew the math. . . .

We'd have to do something.

Then one day I saw the math. And it was my turn. To do something.

That was the day I decided to move out. My first waking thought that day was to see how many fights we actually had since I started keeping track. I really had no idea what I would find. It was more of a curiosity. So I did a quick search on the tag "fight." That's when I knew.

I didn't wake up with the idea that I was going to move out that day. I woke up with the idea to do some math.

The math was displayed like a grade on a high school algebra test. In the 120 weeks preceding that day, I instantly saw that we had 73 fights. That's 73 / 120 weeks. That's a fight about every 10 days or so. And I'm talking a big fight. Not a little argument. I never wrote about those. I only wrote about the life sucking, vein popping, 'round and 'rounds that went on for hours and hours, always resulting in a meltdown of exhaustion, collapsing both of us while resolving nothing.

But there's more.

Each fight was followed by three to four "fight continued" days. Those were the silent standoff days that permeated our every moment with a black cloud. My productivity derailed while I went through the motions half sucking it up and half falling apart inside, until finally, I would just get tired of being mad and pivot back to life and we'd both move on until the next go 'round.

Idea. Agreement. Hope. Hope dashed. Battle. Repeat.

Neither of us were in a good place. We were both suffering at the hands of the one we loved the most.

But Something Just Clicked that morning when I saw the

math and realized the odds weren't in my favor.

I couldn't possibly unsee what was clearly and logically screaming before my eyes. I had to choose to leave. We ran out the clock on our chances. The timing just wasn't right for us anymore.

Repeating the same and expecting different results was insanity.

Defined.

Chapter 8

High Dives

Along the way to the D word, I was completely unaware of the whole process. Or even that I was really in the process. Even with my gut as a guide, I never fully accepted that divorce would actually be a thing for us, because after all, it wasn't Me. I wasn't the divorcing type. And it wasn't Us. We weren't the divorcing type. We were special. We would get through this. We weren't like other mortal couples. We made it through raising and homeschooling a bunch of kids plus building businesses and houses, remodeling rental properties, surviving financial meltdowns, job losses and more.

We were special all right.

But that didn't mean we were immune to irreconcilable differences.

From the time I popped out the D word on our front porch that beautiful spring morning, I never really believed it would happen. It was like how I felt with all four of my pregnancies. Like the inevitable wasn't going to happen. As in literally having a relatively large human come out of me. That really wasn't going to happen to me. . . .

I think that's the other D word. Denial at its best.

Denial is a special super power we have as humans that allows us to turn the volume down on the scary so we can keep moving forward.

Then suddenly, out of the blue, there you are. Facing the biggest cringeworthy, toe curling thing you've ever had to do. And you want nothing of it, but there's no way out. You've done all the things to get you to that spot, getting closer and closer to that most logical conclusion and now was the time. You needed to push that baby out. No one else could do that for you.

So you roll up your sleeves and do what you need to do. In that moment that has finally come.

The only thing to do now is take that one step off the proverbial high dive. Like it or not, you can't crawl down the ladder any more.

So I jumped. And I survived. I told my husband I wanted a divorce.

Then I realized my first jump was just a warm up. As with most big things in life, they require big leaps. And lots of them.

And the D word is no exception.

It's often said that if we knew then what we know now, we'd probably never do some of the things we've done.

But I think we would. We don't choose our big things based on how hard they are to achieve. That's all blurred behind some magic screen for us to deal with later. (That's where babies come from. . . .)

Divorce is like that. When finally chosen, the pain a person is in drowns out any kind of warnings about the challenges that are to come.

And when the high dives of divorce start being revealed, you begin to see the leaps take on a bunch of different forms. Sometimes we frantically race to the end of the board and jump off as fast as we can to get it over with quickly. Other times we belabor each rung up the ladder, walking tentatively to the end of the board until some force beyond our comprehension pushes us.

With each leap though, we surprise ourselves. We walk away with a little more confidence and even a spring in our step. With each jump, we peek in our rearview mirror and say, "DANG! I can't believe what just happened—what I just did!" And just like that, with a feeling of accomplishment, pride and strength, baby number two is on board before you know it.

But it never gets easier. These jumps.

Denial and amnesia are a great pairing.

With all my beliefs surrounding marriage being forever, I was full up in denial. But surprisingly I wasn't paralyzed by fear. I faced and made those big jumps. In hindsight, I think that's where my solitude paid off. I didn't seek approval, affirmation or advice from anyone which freed me from the danger of second guessing myself. Other than the healthy release of fear to my therapist every now and then, I let my gut and common sense be my guide. Pretty much every trip off the high dive was an unscheduled, spontaneous event. That saved me a lot of anguish. Seriously. When I was ready to jump, each time it was close to effortless—propelled with a nothing-could-stop-me momentum.

The process was never straightforward though. It was a strange mix of anxiety and determination. Each jump held its own special wincing, but nothing that a lot—and I mean a LOT—of deep breaths couldn't manage.

The Jumps

Getting unmarried creates all sorts of terrifying conversations in our heads. We get sucked into all sorts of nonsense that our gremlins chatter on about, creating a picture of drama way worse than it actually is, or ever becomes.

That's how we humans roll.

But that brings up the most important tool I had going through this process: meditation.

If you've never tried it, like I hadn't, it's these impossible-to-imagine things in life that really bring you to your knees and finally put you cross-legged in a picture perfect meditation pose, without any complaints, because after all, you've tried everything else.

Also pushing me to meditate was some cool science I learned along the way. When I discovered that meditating literally changes your brain (in a good way) I couldn't NOT give my inner yogi a serious try. According to Kelly McGonigal in her book *The Willpower Instinct*, research has shown that mediating actually builds up the prefrontal cortex of our brains. Considering that the prefrontal cortex is responsible for our ability to reason and make balanced choices, this news was all too real for me to ignore. I had to try, and I'm glad I've stuck with it.

Meditating has been my greatest tool in what proved to be the most difficult thing I've ever done in my life: UnMarrying My Best Friend.

I highly recommend it. (Meditating, that is.)

On the way to the diving board multiple times, I would often dart back to the side of the pool deck to meditate first. I'd escape on long walks or bike rides. Or I'd just stop and drop whatever I was doing, plop down, close my eyes and breathe myself back into balance for a few minutes. I needed to get outta my head. Get out of my own way. Clear the cobwebs. And figure out what I really wanted to do at that moment while finding the strength I needed to actually do it.

No one could do that for me. No amount of therapy, self-help books, inspiring memes or happy hours with friends could get me off that diving board.

Only I could make the leaps.

What follows is a peek into my many high dive moments. It

will either scare you away from the thought of unmarrying, or give you peace in knowing that all these jumps are survivable. Icky yes, but they won't kill you.

And hopefully, if unmarrying is actually a real consideration for you, you'll be able to safely and temporarily hunker down in your own denial so you can get some sleep tonight and deal with it tomorrow. :)

Chapter 9

Separating

The Warmup

My trip to the front porch that spring morning didn't come out of nowhere. It was years in the making. Through our shared adventure, my husband and I made many mistakes, took countless missteps and suffered through many unfortunate events. Some marriages can survive this and others can't. On my way to unmarrying my best friend, I did everything I could for us to be the former. But sadly, in the end, each of our best efforts wasn't enough to keep us away from the courthouse steps.

It took many steps to get there though. It's not like in the movies where the couple decides to get divorced and that's that. It's all kinds of squeamish icky that no one wants to go near but there's no other way out. One heart stopping, anxiety riddled conversation after the next with people known and never known, stirring up a reality smacking identity crisis that makes you feel like you're sidelined as a spectator to all the world living their best life.

But you gotta break some eggs to make an omelette even if you don't have an appetite.

One of the first biggest moves I made was to separate in the house. I consider this my warmup leap on a smaller diving board. It was real. It was hard. And it was a turning point.

Like most of my trips off the high dive though, it came on spontaneously and was executed in the whirling dervish style of effortless. At some point, you just crack through the thoughts and talks in your head, and follow through with action. I had been noodling around with this idea of separating for over a year. I never wanted to do it and avoided going down that path as much as possible. Remember, I'm the one who LOVED sleeping with my husband. My comfort was in our bed, entwined like pretzels, heart to heart.

But the stressors proved too much for me to look away anymore. I was walking with so much imbalance and my body was showing it as the years piled on. First with multiple ulcers and then with a poster child's case of shingles. Plus an over all—what I recognize now as—depression that derailed my productivity at every turn. Just when I'd feel invincible and balanced, we'd have at it with another battle and off the beam I would tumble, wasting way too many days trying to recover.

Separating in the house would help, I thought. To me it held two purposes. One, to provide me much needed peace. And two, to hopefully punctuate the severity of our issues so I could be met with some like-minded get'r done from my husband. We had lots of work to do and I couldn't do it alone.

As I mentioned before, my husband said this was the move that killed our marriage.

And indeed it was. It was the beginning of the end.

It didn't have to be the end though. From my back porch, I still believe it could have been therapeutic for both of us. Especially considering staying in our bedroom was not an option for me. I couldn't continue doing the same thing hoping for different results.

But neither his story nor my story matter at the end of the day. They are 180 degrees apart. Seen through entirely different lenses. Irreconcilable.

It happened in the blurry-eyed silence and reprieve of another bitter battle. He had retreated as he normally would. Stepping over the body, as I called it, giving me the needed space I never wanted. The walk-away that keeps on giving. It only shoves the problem under the bed to predictably appear time and time again. All the while I carried around a rapidly growing resentment that festered into a fog of undeniable pain I fought to disguise.

I wanted to face our demons. He didn't.

But I'm not saying that when I pushed us to face the demons that it was either pretty or that it helped us in the long run. At times, along the way to this unmarrying, I've thought he was probably right to just shove the problems under the bed—and I could've / should've just walked away without a fight. Surrender and leave.

That is, if I really wanted to accept my situation the way it was. But I wasn't willing to do that. I just couldn't accept that there wasn't a better Us in us.

Ultimately, we each put up a good fight to save Us. We tried with all our might—and that looked different for each of us.

But until then, I thought separating in the house might/could help. So one night after a long tension-filled day of ignoring each other, some wild inspiration walked me down to the basement to just look around.

And that's when I got all creative.

Why couldn't I? Why couldn't I just move my stuff down here and see if this works? I couldn't go another night lying beside him with this tension between us. Our bed. Our sanctuary of peace. A place we're both most vulnerable. I just couldn't.

I decided I had nothing to lose. I decided not to make a scene. I decided not to ask him to leave. I decided since I was the one wanting out, he shouldn't have to leave the comfort of his lair.

I started slowly. Moving one piece of junk to one side of the room, throwing another piece out, etc etc etc, until this lonely basement room we called The Ruins started to look like I could make it a home after all. I calmly toted my belongings, armful by armful down the two flights of stairs, passing him more times than not.

At first his silence was unremarkable.

Then as the hours marched on, the gremlins in my head got louder and louder. Gone was the calm decent to the basement of my peace. Reminding me with every trip up and down the stairs, all I was hearing inside was, "I told you so. I told you he wouldn't say a thing. Or do a thing. Or try to help you. Or try to stop you. Or even try to save Us."

Then snap! While trying to muscle a broken sofa bed into place, I knew I had more than I could physically bear. I'm tough, but not that tough. I cussed and cried to an empty room. Picking myself up from a puddle of pity, I tore up the stairs and snarled and screamed for help.

Welcome to my full-blown Gremlin Show. Out they came like an ugly chorus, letting everyone know who was calling the shots now.

In the blur that followed, I don't remember who was home to hear all this or how it all exactly played out, but my husband did end up helping me get the couch in place. Then he walked away.

The punctuation that I had originally hoped would calmly end with a bittersweet period of reconciliation, ultimately ended with an energy sapping exclamation point of heart-breaking nothingness.

End of warm ups.

The next eight months of separation prepared me for my first no-turning-back trip off the high dive when I broached a $99 Divorce on that beautiful spring morning.

Chapter 10

Therapy

I was a swimmer in high school so it was only natural that one of my first jobs was as a lifeguard and swimming teacher. One of the coolest things I remember growing up was the outdoor municipal pool. It had a high dive which was rare back then, and virtually extinct now. I didn't realize at the time how lucky I was to have access to such a thrill, but I sure loved it.

The pool was located on a major state road connecting our little suburban bubble to the rest of the Twin Cities of Minneapolis / St Paul, so every time we went anywhere, we drove by that pool. And every time we did, I made sure I took a peek at that high dive beckoning me on the side of the road. In winter, I dreamed of summer, and in summer, I waited in sweaty lines to find my way into that chlorine pond.

By high school, I was ecstatic to get behind the scenes as a lifeguard. That's when I observed all the different techniques in launching off that diving board in the sky. Sitting atop the lifeguard stand, feeling the status of a knighted royal, baking in the Minnesota summer sun, I saw that not all kids embraced the high dive like I did.

Everyone had their own style. Some would run like crazy pants off the end, others would cling to the end of the platform with shivering fright, and a select few superstars would bounce gracefully then soar with gravity while rolling beautiful twists and turns.

And then there were the frustrating ones who would hold up the line, gingerly taking one painfully slow step up the ladder at a time, as if holding off the inevitable would change their decent.

This is what my trip off the high dive to therapy looked like.

Not only did I fear it, I didn't think I needed it.

Terror and denial. A deadly combination.

When I extracted myself out of our bedroom and separated in the house, I told my husband we needed professional help. I bravely launched that proclamation because I knew he wouldn't go for it.

I wasn't surprised. He said no. So I didn't put up a fight.

I could easily say, (and have said) "I tried to get him to go....."

But really. I didn't try that hard.

I didn't want to go anymore than he did.

And besides. I knew what was wrong with him. With me. And with us. I had that all dialed in, I thought. And better yet, I knew how to fix us.

Cuz I'm a fixer.

Do-It-Yourself Girl to the core, I figured out a plan. And I still believe that if my DIY Therapy plan was followed through to fruition, we would've made it to the other side of our problems and I'd be writing a completely different book.

My simple plan included developing daily habits for reflection, awareness and growth. Each day required meditating, reading, reflecting and sharing. None of the "things" were terribly difficult, but doing them consistently would require discipline.

Above all, I figured these habits would be good for any human, whether it saved our marriage or not. Who couldn't use more strength in these areas? I may have never gone to traditional therapy, but I had a strong hunch it wasn't a silver bullet. It would require homework, so why not just do the work?

I knew my DIY Therapy plan would be an uphill climb for my husband though. For years I tried to get him on board with my airy fairy ideas, but he just bobble-headed me. When I'd talk about relationship issues or things I had read and learned, he mostly just bobbled his head like a little toy doll on the dashboard of a car. Sort of in agreement. Not a solid yes. Not a solid no. It would slide in one ear and out the other. Nothing would change.

This time though, the stakes were higher. I had never been so close to a door I didn't want to walk through. I desperately wanted this new plan to work, but I had enough respect for myself that if he didn't follow through with his commitment to our plan, then it was over. I couldn't continue without him showing me that he would work with me to help save our marriage.

Any good plan plans for failure and that's where I knew we'd have problems. Follow through was his Achilles heal. So, I made sure he understood how serious the stakes were and included a zero-strikes-you're-out policy. Remember, the odds weren't in my favor. I was burning daylight. I wasn't going to risk one more do-over.

The plan was a 90 day commitment of two hours a day; one hour of homework and one hour of sharing with each other. The homework consisted of reading growth material for 30 minutes, mediating for 10 minutes and writing / reflecting for another 10 to 20 minutes a day. Then we would just talk about it.

The 90 days was completely arbitrary and spontaneously created by me on the fly. I figured it worked for warranties, it could work for us.

For three weeks we soared! For the first 21 days he showed up, listened and participated. Every single day we read, talked, hashed things out, screamed and cried, for at least three hours a day. Yes, imagine that! We did more than planned and I felt like we both were enjoying it. We would meet in my room at 7 am and many times he wouldn't leave until nearly noon. I didn't trap him in the room. He chose to stay and continue.

At times it was really painful for both of us, but at other times it was soul-stirringly amazing. And as the days rolled on it seemed to get better and better. Ironically, I had never felt as connected to him as I did at that time in our marriage. I really thought we could pull it off. I really felt hopeful about our marriage.

But then I had to go out of town. I made adjustments so that we could meet via FaceTime. The key is consistency. In order to make a solid change in lifestyle, you need to stay committed to your new routine for a good period of time in order to form a new habit. Research has shown a minimum of six weeks to several months is needed.

After three weeks of significant progress, we were at a point where I needed him to start taking initiative rather than me being the one leading all the time. I was very much in the therapist role. It's unsustainable to be a romantic partner and a therapist at the same time. One of our biggest problems in our marriage had been me feeling like I was the one pulling the plow all by myself. I told him we could even have abbreviated sessions. He bobble-headed agreed.

Considering unavoidable travel, all I required was for him to call me. At 7 am. We would meet for no more than one hour. I promised to be there.

And that's when our house of cards started tumbling down.

He never called.

Back to the usual.

Idea. Agreement. Hope. Hope dashed. Battle.

Giving him the benefit of the doubt, I came home from my four day trip, saddened, but hopeful that he would meet me with something. Anything. Any sort of work around to show initiative.

Crickets. Nothing. Not even a mention that he didn't call me.

And from that point on, my ideas went a whole different direction. . . .

Seven months later we were on the front porch and I launched the D word, taking my first trip off the high dive.

Soon to follow was the realization that real therapy would probably be a good idea for me at this point.

The idea of therapy was still excruciating, but I was so far gone, depressed, empty and lost, I really had nothing to lose. I was stuck and didn't know how to get out of my box. I didn't talk to my mom. I didn't talk to any of my friends. I walked with this monster in my head every single step of the day.

By now, my slow accent to the top of the high dive was complete. Now I needed to find a therapist. I finally resolved to pony up the cash to get myself some help, which made me cringe. Money was usually my first excuse to not follow through. Once past that objection, who could I trust? That was my second biggest holdup. Certainly they were all going to mess with my head. So I did what any wise woman would do. I talked to my hairstylist; she had been my surrogate therapist for over a decade. I knew I could trust her referral.

I held onto his number for a couple weeks and finally made the call. With pulse racing, script planned, I blurted out a general request for an appointment, ready for the twenty questions that I imagined would follow. To my surprise, no questions were asked other than when and what time?

The appointment day arrived and I was now at the end of the diving board. Now I just had to get to the appointment.

As I prepared to leave that morning, I moved through my usual hustle out the door with an unusual and calming 15 minutes to spare. I left with plenty of time to wheel through Starbucks and make the 45 minute trip at a peaceful pace. The whole time, reciting the bundle of words I would say at the therapist's presumed question, "Why are you here?"

With the nerves of a high school kid waiting to give her first speech, I pulled the door open to his office and was greeted with a warm smile and invited to sit down. I could do this, I said to myself as I silently breathed in anxiously.

I sat down. He sat down. He asked nothing. He said nothing.

Then out came all my words that had been trapped inside me for decades. . . .

Into the pool I went.

At the end of that first session, the therapist asked me what I feared about coming to the appointment. After an hour of word vomiting, my authenticity was primed. I felt safe to reflect and express.

Judgement, I said. I was afraid of his judgement.

I knew how irrational that was, making it even more humiliating to share. He was a therapist. It was his job to listen and help. Not to judge. But not even that could convince my menacing gremlins to stand down.

Shame only on to them. Those gremlins. They are not me.

That trip off the high dive into therapy was one of the best things I did for myself along the way. Looking back, it took me out of "stuck" and moved me into "growth." I didn't go to therapy a lot; just a couple times a month for a few months and then when needed, off and on, until the divorce was final.

For such a DIY girl, I'm not only proud of myself that I made this jump into therapy, I'm truly grateful for my therapist. He didn't try to fix me or tell me what to do. I still had to do the work myself. But he provided a safe space for me to say the things I needed to say, but couldn't and wouldn't say to anyone. All the while he patiently helped me stay the course, guiding me wherever I decided I needed to go.

Lookback

When I finished writing this chapter, I asked myself the obvious. What if we had gone to therapy instead of doing my DIY therapy? Do I think it would have saved us?

Maybe. Maybe not. Knowing my husband and the headspace he was in at the time, I don't think even a therapist could have convinced him to do the work. My guess is we would've ended up in the same place. We will never know.

But I do know had I gone to therapy myself a year earlier, it would've saved me from a lot of pain. And I probably would have moved through the process with a lot more grace and caused a lot less fallout for everyone.

Growth wrapped in discomfort.

Jump.

Chapter 11

The Mad Dash: Moving out

I never dreamed of getting divorced. Who does? What I mean is, that in the 18 months or so that lead to our final divorce hearing, I wasn't conjuring up divorce as my dreamy end result. I really didn't see it as a reality until about four or five days before I filed. And even then, I held my breath. . . .

I dreamed of peace. Calm. Connection. Fulfillment.

I was raised by a strong and brilliant woman who planted the seed in my little mind that our dreams were always within reach. With that pocketful of sunshine embedded in my heart, I was wide-open minded to the whole starry eyed manifesting idea. As I set out into adulthood, I became more and more wise to the details of how all this dreamy stuff worked. And it kept proving itself true throughout my life.

So why in the world would I choose to go through a divorce—arguably one of the worst life experiences to endure—if I was such a manifesting machine?

Because, I learned, sometimes on the way to a dream, twists and turns are unavoidable. And the more we avoid and deny the obstacles, the longer it takes to reach our dreamy dreams.

I could argue with myself that had I been clearer with what I really wanted earlier in our marriage, I may not have had to go through such suffering. Either we could have fixed a lot of the trouble spots in our marriage, and in ourselves, in their infancy, or we would've/could've cut bait sooner.

But I can't really blame myself for being a Queen of Denial. Looking back, I don't believe any mirror-in-the-face moment would have derailed our journey to building a family together. That was the bigger dream at the time.

Either way, denial clearly is a wolf in sheep's clothing.

And when they say be careful what you wish for, I think they're talking about all the mayhem we face while deep in manifesting mania. On my way to Peace, sometimes it felt like I was on a black diamond slope to hell, but surprising to me was that I always found my way to the chalet to warm up and catch my breath before my next trip up the mountain. Or high dive. Same same.

One day, a few months after beginning therapy, and another ultimatum beyond, I was startled to find myself channeling the kid running crazy pants off the end of that diving board in the sky. Weighing heavily on my mind was that little bit of math I mentioned a few chapters ago.

The math of risk /reward was hollering at me.

I take my first morning thoughts very seriously. When I say, "So this morning, when I first woke up, I was thinking . . .," my people know it means I'm likely hatching something.

That morning I woke up to the tiny whisper, "I wonder how many fights we've had . . ." My agenda for the day started with an appointment with my therapist. A few days prior, my husband had asked me if he could come to my appointment with me. The ask wasn't as straightforward as that, but I won't belabor the story with the battle that preceded or ensued. Suffice it to say, he was coming along to my appointment, at his request.

And no, you can't ride with me. . . .

As I was getting ready to go, something nudged me to go back into my bedroom and get the clipboard that held my morning math. The data I computed had slapped me in the face and was dying for attention. Maybe it should come with me, I thought.

I arrived at the appointment a few minutes early with enough space to catch my breath for what, I had no idea. Chip on my shoulder and harboring my angst with each measured breath, I rolled my eyes as my husband rolled in frantically, on time to the last second. We exchanged painful, fear-filled fake pleasantries and awkwardly shuttled into the therapist's office, one after the other.

What followed was a session-filled flurry of spontaneous and bottled up badness that clearly displayed our messed up Us-ness. My Mad Dash Move Out had just begun and I didn't even know it.

My only plan going into this appointment was to say

Not-A-Word. To let my husband speak his mind while I stood down in my calm, untriggered peace.

A girl can wish.

Part of that happened. I stood down, but untriggered and wordless I was not. I swallowed my fury and let it out in calm, measured bits and nods. And then without notice, out popped my clipboard, jumping into the hands of the therapist, with an introduction of how my data-driven husband would be appreciative of this math.

My therapist howled. I cringed. What was he laughing at?!

I explained the math. For more than two years, we lived through 73 weeks of serious fighting. That's a big battle every couple weeks. Each lasting a good three to four days. And that's just when I started keeping track. There were many years before that looked the same—before I got the idea to keep track. Surely this quantifiable data had to validate my pain, right? Why was he laughing?

"Never in my 40 years of experience," my therapist said, 'have I ever seen such data from a client. This is good. Really good," he laughed.

I was relieved.

Then horrified.

"Now what?" I thought.

He asked me if there was anything my husband could do to fix this.

I shook a fervent no.

My husband pushed, incredulously blurting out if that

meant I wanted a divorce.

I said yes.

He fumed, "Then let's get this done today."

I calmly and confidently obliged.

"Ok let's."

The next thing I remember is him hurrying out of the building. All this neatly ended our hour-long session. I followed a few paces behind him after exchanging a glance of Oh My God with my therapist. That one glance said it all. Something big just happened.

As I got into my car, my husband pleaded with me.

I couldn't.

I wouldn't.

And I didn't.

I don't know if I said anything to him or not at that point. I just remember getting into the car, putting on my seatbelt, backing out and driving off. About 10 minutes into the drive I found myself at the end of a high dive I didn't even realize I had climbed.

Something Just Clicked.

I couldn't stay in the house anymore. Regardless of how big our house was, not even our little town seemed big enough to separate me from the darkness that had become our marriage; what was supposed to be the sanctuary of my peace.

I had planned to pick my mom up after my therapy appointment to take her on a few errands. At 86 years old, she and I made the rounds together all the time. I love every minute with my mom, and treasure it like it's the last. Being with her is a joy; she has always been my biggest fan, and I likewise.

But as things got more difficult in my marriage I held back sharing my dramas with her. Although I told her I separated in the house, and even told her about our DIY Therapy, I kept her free from the story as it unfolded. Although she would've provided me much appreciated moral support, it was entirely a ME thing. What I was going through was so huge and life sucking, I needed all the energy I could muster to just process it on a daily basis. I withheld to preserve my own stamina.

I picked my mom up on the way back from my appointment. We had to go to the bank then do a couple other errands. As we sat with the personal banker, I worried that the unease I felt was clearly written all over my face. I didn't want my mom to pick up any of my feels. She's razor sharp on anything in that department. I went through the motions like we do when being inauthentic, talking about the weather and other superficial things.

We got to the car and I suggested we go out to lunch. My mom is always up for going out to lunch with me; we have racked up a lifetime of the most amazing memories going out to lunch, sharing a glass of wine or two.

I knew this one would be for the records.

We went to our favorite restaurant and were handed menus then ordered our wine. It was all that I could do to smile through the process and pinch in the tears that were piling up behind my eyes.

Wouldn't you know, when you have the biggest things in life to share, you have the most attentive waiter. Argh.

I finally found an opening. Waiter gone.

I'm going to leave him, I said.

My mom just said, Ok.

I wasn't sure if she heard me.

I said it again.

She said, yes. I heard. This is good, Maria.

And then out came the tears. And yes the waiter too. Double argh.

I asked if I could move in with her. I couldn't stay in our house any more. It was completely clear to me now that nothing would ever change. I had to leave. I couldn't stay in our house, dodging the demons that reside. I had no thought or plan or any idea what the future would hold for me, let alone that I was closer to the dreaded D word than ever.

All I knew was that I had to leave.

After lunch I dropped my mom off at her house and took my last turn into our driveway as a resident of the house we designed, built and then raised our family in for 22 years. Crossing the threshold of this lifelong dream would never be the same.

But I wasn't thinking of any of that in the moment.

I parked the car. Got out quickly. Hustled to my bedroom and made the fastest mad dash out of there as I could. My husband worked at home and was in another part of the house so the last thing I wanted was to meet him in flight. Within about 20 minutes I stuffed a couple suitcases and a Hefty bag full of whatever I imagined a run-a-way would need.

Within minutes I was a mile away, on my mom's doorstep. As I trudged one load in after another, I thanked her, and we laughed at the tragic thought that this morning neither one of us had any idea that I would become her roommate that day.

Crazy pants dash to the end of the diving board. Splash!

What I've learned on this journey to divorce is that every painful and ugly step along the way was so necessary to bring me to the place of peace I'm at right now as I write this. I needed to walk down every single twisted path, leading from one high dive to another, to really know my next step.

And with each bounce off that board, I got better at making the leap. Trust and faith piled on.

Chapter 12

The Asset Talk

It's weird how some of the most significant moments in life seem so random. Without any of the anticipation of a graduation or a child's birth, but carry with them the same weighty meaning. That's what moving out was to me. Completely random, and only predictable in hindsight.

What followed after I landed on my mom's doorstep that afternoon added even more spice to that day's significance.

With the energy of a triage nurse, I spent the next hour or so transforming my mom's guest room for the uncertain future. I'm not sure if rapid nesting is special to me, my gender, or our species, but at this time of chaos, I had a full helping of get'r done. One thing I noticed about myself in these dark years of uncoupling was that physical labor helped me through my bleakest of days. Folding laundry, sweeping, cleaning the pool, washing down the porch. Anything that required no decision making or thought to accomplish the task. A sort of meditation that serves up some needed endorphins and feelings of accomplishment.

But this productive tidal wave was different. I wasn't depressed. I was too scared to be depressed. I was in escape mode, running for my life. I needed to do anything I could to avoid terrifying looks into the future, or gut punching peeks at the past. Setting up my new nest at my mom's was automatic. I could've crashed on the bed in the fetal position and cried my eyes out, but the tsunami inside me moved me otherwise. Without realizing it, I was doing exactly what I needed to do to get through these excruciating moments. No amount of help from anyone could get me through this experience. This was an island moment.

Not surprisingly though, in all this ruckus, I forgot a few items in my haste to leave our house. So, without a thought, I drove over, hustled in and out with a sprawling armful of stuff, got in the car, and put it in gear.

That's when it hit me. Like the sun popping out between a sky of endless angry clouds. I was free. Not free as in a prisoner just released. But free from the hopelessness that dragged me down for years. Just like that. Like a switch.

A year before, when I separated in the house, the switch flipped to a taste of peace.

When I moved out of the house, the switch flipped to a taste of hope.

But it was just a little taste. Not a Herculean dose. But enough to rouse up a giddy inside me like a new teenage driver. That first-drive-out-the-driveway-alone kind of glee that's mixed with caution at every tentative turn.

Short-lived as this glee was, the calming feeling of hope never abated. It only got bigger and bigger, powering me through all the necessary and nerve-wracking trips up the high dive that followed.

The next four months were filled with all sorts of darkness though, and lots of indefinites. I didn't focus on what came next in the long, or even short run. I mostly focused on what monsters lay before me in the moment. Minute by minute, hour by hour, day by day. Many days I found myself counting the hours down to when I could go to bed.

But something just clicked on Thanksgiving morning. Again, I found myself facing a high dive I didn't see coming when I put my feet on the floor that morning.

Thanksgiving has always been a big deal with our family. A kick off to the holiday season, it naturally primed our family for the togetherness that makes this time of year so magical. But this year, it was not only a wild card, I was in deep denial of it's arrival. It wasn't until two days before that I realized I needed to make a decision on what we were going to do. Turkey issues push you to face reality. The bird needed a couple days to thaw.

I decided we would do a very simple Thanksgiving dinner with just our kids and my mom and her guy George. And yes that included my husband. Throughout this process, he and I continued to carry on with the business of family and finances as usual and as needed. The only real difference with our day-to-day, other than the tension and awkwardness between us, was that we didn't live together. Even to this day, a few months post divorce, I find it interesting how we can move back and forth from emotionally driven relationship dramas to all business. Like a switch.

On Thanksgiving morning, I went over to the house early so I could get the meal rolling and clean the house. As my coffee started to download in my body, the powerful inspiration that follows began to take over. Often when I'm under an intense deadline, I take on monumental tasks, like cleaning a closet that's been overlooked for years, or painting a wall, or some other irrelevant we-ain't-got-no-time-for-that-kind-of-project project. And strangely, everything always gets done on time, even with all the fur flying. (But I definitely don't recommend it.)

This time, my irrelevant project just happened to be our finances. Because what better time to bring up the division of our assets than Thanksgiving morning?

This was a high dive moment I had no idea was about to happen. I dreaded the idea of all that was involved in dividing our assets from the moment the bitter word 'divorce' crossed my lips. I never went near it. Couldn't and wouldn't imagine it. Yes, I had moved out. And yes, I found peace and calm in my mom's adorable Gnome room, an attic-like space she painted into a fairy garden of love and warmth. And yes, my one and only dream was to live a peaceful life in a deeply connected, intimate relationship with a life-long partner who clearly wasn't proving to be my husband.

But I just couldn't imagine dealing with the real business of divorce.

A friend of mine told me divorce is all about the finances. I disagreed. To me it was all about a release of the emotional handcuffs. That's where I was coming from; but thankfully, the gods of Deal With Reality propelled me up the high dive that Thanksgiving morning, pushing me to face the reality of the nitty gritty.

I texted my husband. I knew he was in the basement. He works nights, so waking him at 8 am to talk about the division of assets on Thanksgiving morning was a superb idea.

He came upstairs blurry eyed and unamused at my invitation. I made him some coffee. We sat at the kitchen table and started a civilized conversation, ignoring the pain in each other's eyes.

We don't have a lot of assets, but we have some real estate. That makes our sort of simple situation a little complicated. But to me, it seemed straightforward. In literally 10 seconds I scratched out a handwritten spreadsheet divided into his and mine. I quickly Zillow'd appraisals of each property and sorted them out in equal measures as much as possible.

Well. That certainly wasn't that. . . .

The battle began.

The simple math problem that I had seen became an emotionally driven smack down that had nothing to do with our assets and everything to do with me being a quitter and him not wanting the divorce in the first place.

He triggered. Then I triggered. The fur flew. Wildly.

And the windows were open.

Nice job, Maria. Good time to bring this all up. Face palm.

The next thing I knew I was flying out the front door, cancelling Thanksgiving.

Yes. Even better. Way to go Maria.

The thing about these high dives is that sometimes they end in a belly flop. I crash landed us into the guts of divorce with a cup of coffee and a piece of scratch paper. On a major holiday.

I wouldn't recommend.

But it got the ball rolling.

After that wicked battle, out of my mind and raw from the mind-boggling reality that my world was crashing at my own doing, I fled on foot. I walked. And walked. Then I biked. All over town. All day. Until finally resting my bewilderment in a hammock at a lake side park, drowning in tears of sorrow that seemed to have no end in sight. I finished this pitiful day sharing a take-out Thanksgiving dinner from Denny's with my mom.

Negotiations had officially begun.

But I knew we couldn't see or speak to each other until we reached an overall agreement on our finances. I only wanted to communicate via text. No meetings with sounds or flesh.

Over the years, texting had saved us from a lot of trouble in our relationship. Back in the day it was called IM-ing. My husband and I have avoided many loud and feisty encounters, saving our kids from lots of painful squabbles, with hands on the keyboard rather than around each other's necks.

Texting can definitely kill a relationship, but when it's already on its deathbed, texting can keep things much more civil. For one thing, you have to be on better behavior because texts are forever. You can't get caught in he said she said stuff because it's right there in front of you. It's also less energy sapping and you can control your triggers a little better. It isn't perfect. And we all know snarky flows just as effortlessly with 26 letters as with a million spoken words, but it definitely slows your roll.

So at this point in our unmarrying process, I knew I didn't have the stamina for the wild card of face-to-face, or even audio communication. We needed to have our heads about us to deal with the reality we faced. Anything beyond the sterile words in text would be way too emotionally charged.

We went through several weeks of 'round and 'round. But it was never entirely financially focused which dragged it out and made it all the worse. Monsters, hurts and disappointments still bubbled up, even behind the veil of texting. I was to the point of telling him I didn't care. Just come up with something, I said.

Finally he came back with a plan that pretty much exactly resembled my scratched out plan from Thanksgiving.

The thing about my ex is that he may be driven by the F word of Fear a lot of the times, but one thing that's always been solid with him is his deep respect for the other F-word: Fair. He made sure our kids were raised to never to say this F-word at home...as in Life's Not Fair. But, when it can be, he makes sure it is.

Another reason I love this man, and why unmarrying him was so hard.

Even though these negotiations were brutal, we both survived. It didn't kill us, as most things don't.

After all this, I realized, my friend was right to some degree. Divorce might literally be all about finances; dividing assets. But figuratively it's not about the money. It never is.

Chapter 13

Humiliation and a $299 Divorce

Now that we made a big picture decision on the asset division, we could deal with the details in person, I thought. Certainly we should be able to handle that, right? I made it clear that this was not a time to talk about our unsolvable relationship issues, and if our conversation headed in that direction, I would leave.

Easier said than done.

It's tricky to separate the dollars from the disappointment you feel when unmarrying. Regular relationship breakups are hard enough. But they generally don't create major threats to your financial security. The security that marriage provides is felt in opposite and equal measures when taken away. From secure to insecure in one swift jump. Keeping your wits about you when those fears run wild in your head is tough.

I knew if we could get past the money part, we would be ok. Our kids were all grown. Aged 20-22-24 and 26, they were all leading independent lives. That's not to say they weren't emotionally crushed by our break up, but at least we had moved past the milestone of raising them, which ultimately made the nitty gritty of the divorce process so much less complicated.

We met at Starbucks, a neutral place where I thought we would be more mindful of our ugly triggered gremlins. . . .

Over the years, Starbucks has become my second office. My work travels with me in my backpack. I can work anywhere as long as I have my laptop and internet. It's nice to get out of the house for a change of scenery and to see humans. I've gotten a lot accomplished in this coffee shop. And while going through the unmarrying process, it has also brought a lot of happy light into my life during this really dark and isolating time.

I have become a regular at two nearby locations, spending enough time at both that most of the employees not only know my name, but my order before I even say a word. And just as they've gotten to know my habits, I've gotten to know their customers' habits. If someone hasn't written a book about the customers of Starbucks, they should. In my hundreds of hours sipping coffee and tapping away on my laptop, I've observed all sorts of life events, transitions and transactions. Job interviews, job losses, buying a home, selling a home, wedding planning, estate planning, new friends, old friends, first dates, last dates, newly marrieds, long time marrieds and even clandestine and married to others.

And so much more going on just inches apart, table upon table. Life coming and going. All over a cup of brew.

You don't realize how your stuff stands out so clearly even

when buried in the buzz of the caffeinated clatter.

Until someone tells you. . . .

We were sitting in the back. My favorite spot. The last table and near the bathrooms. I always situate myself so I can see people coming and going. I always want to be backed up to the view. The small rectangular four-person tables aren't quite big enough to feel comfortable with dueling laptops face to face, so sitting diagonal to one another is preferred. The conversation my husband and I were having though, didn't require our laptops, but we sat diagonal from each other anyway. Face to face seemed just too brutal that day, which was sad to me, and felt strongly. We have always felt closest when sitting directly across from each other so we can look into each other's eyes when talking. We've never been the couple that sits alongside each other in a restaurant.

This was the beginning of the end of our days of eye contact. When I'm upset with someone, it's really hard for me to look them in the eye. With my husband, now my ex, it continues to be really uncomfortable.

We started the conversation civilly enough. I pulled out my notebook and showed him my tactical scribbles. He made his points. I made my points. The volley started and seemed to be going well, until it started to speed up. Back and forth then getting dangerously close to out of bounds with every shot. In the time it takes to down a half a cup of brew, we were wrestling in the gutter. Back and forth. High shot. Low blow. And everywhere in between. Hours later and forgotten in the dizzy dance of hushed and urgent tones was my broken promise to leave if we got into relationship issues.

We were on the road to nowhere again, and just couldn't right our course. Even with snacks, drink refills and bathroom breaks.

The store emptied out for the most part by mid afternoon, except for a woman sitting facing me at the next table. I kept shushing my husband throughout our mental matchup so she wouldn't make out our words. I didn't think we were doing too badly in that regard, considering how heated we were.

As we carried on, I barely noticed the comings and goings of others around us. But I did notice that the woman next to us was gone. That's good, I thought. Even though we were being quiet, there was a point there when I looked up and caught her gaze. She gave me that, "you poor thing" look, making me squirm.

We continued. One useless point after another. Making no progress. But we kept going. Like we were both hanging on to the last bit of whatever we had together.

Until she returned.

Mid-sentence, I looked up and there she was. The woman who was sitting at the next table was back and now standing at our table awkwardly trying to interrupt us.

"Excuse me," she said cautiously and continued. "I know this is weird, but I was sitting at the next table and I could really feel a lot of negative energy. I couldn't hear what you were talking about, but I could tell you're going through...something...." Her words trailed off into tears and she set a Starbucks gift card on the table. "Take this. It's the least I can do," she said.

I got up and gave her a hug as I fought back my own tears of shame. My husband did likewise.

Gut punch. We just hit one of our lowest lows.

I don't remember what we said to each other after she left, but we soon followed out the door. Tails between our legs.

That moment, something just clicked.

I was done. For good.

I couldn't dance that life sucking-dance of our's any more. I had to pull the plug.

But how?

A few days later I went to the other Starbucks in town. I couldn't bear to go back to the location we were at before. Humiliation is a powerful thing. I wasn't sure what I was going to work on that morning, but in my mind was a huge question mark about how I was going to actually get divorced. It was right before Christmas and I had been determined to get the ball rolling with this divorce before the new year. I didn't want to go through another year in this same pain and limbo. I wanted resolution.

Years ago I picked up a really wise a-ha from Mike Dooley, known for his *Notes From The Universe* and his appearance in *The Secret.* His overriding message is always Thoughts Become Things, with the "cursed hows" being deal killers. He points out that we don't need to know every single How on the journey to our dreams. If you were driving from Orlando to Miami, he says, you know the general direction and the major roadways you need to take, but you don't need to worry about every single exit along the way. The details will unfold as you keep rolling towards your end result.

That Keep Rolling idea has been my compass throughout this unmarrying process. When I'd look too far into the future, I'd find myself overwhelmed by The Hows. The undefinable details and scary what ifs. Then I'd wake up and adjust. Usually with a long walk, bike ride or meditation, my end result would come back into view.

Now I was at a place in my journey where new details needed to be conjured up, so I started digging. Using my common sense it was time for me to figure out how a person literally gets divorced. It was time.

I'm so glad I didn't worry about these details earlier, because they unfolded more effortlessly than I expected.

I started out with a scary-for-me phone call to my mom's estate attorney. I really liked her, but none-the-less, I was ashamed of what I had to ask. I kept my story so close to my vest and away from the real world, the thought of spitting out words about what I needed was nauseating. All those gremlins came out and berated me with shame, but I forged ahead, blowing past their insults.

When looking back at the worries I have had before I make any move, I'm always annoyed that I was scared in the first place. My conversation with the lawyer went perfectly. She was very kind and compassionate. And she gave me the practical information I needed.

Divorce is not cheap. Even an uncontested divorce would be about $7,000 if we only used one lawyer, she told me. And from my research, mediation isn't the thriftiest pathway either, generally coming in at about half the cost of an uncontested divorce after all was said and done.

And then, she said, if my husband were to contest the divorce, it would easily be $20,000 each for starts. We'd both need our own attorney and it would get ugly.

That's all I needed to hear. Deflated? Yes, a bit. But I knew there had to be another way.

I remembered the billboard. The $99 Divorce billboard. What was that all about?

I googled $99 Divorce and BAM! I found all kinds of ideas.

Most started at around $199 to about $799. Online. DIY Divorce. How perfect for us!

There were several companies that offered what I soon figured out was simply a document generation service. I learned that you could manage the paperwork yourself, but these services make it a little bit easier. Kind of like Turbo Tax for divorce.

I'm not an over-analyzer when it comes to making buying decisions, but I did do a good afternoon of due-diligence combing the internet for reviews and ratings. I settled on 3StepDivorce. They seemed to have good ratings and came in at $299. All this is assuming an uncontested divorce. We would still have to pay filing fees and court costs with the county, which would be a few hundred dollars. But over all, it seemed pretty straight forward.

Now. Time to tell my husband.

Climbing up the high dive again. . . .

The last time we had talked was at that unforgettably humiliating Starbucks meeting a few days before. I still cringe about that moment and feel like I should have gone back there to sage the store. UGH.

Now I had to tell my husband it was about to get really real. That I was going to file for divorce, and soon. As in days soon. In looking at the online program, I realized I could get through the paperwork pretty quickly and be filed for divorce by Monday. The day before New Year's Eve.

As soon as I figured out what could actually happen, I called my husband. I didn't wait to think about what I was going to say, knowing I'd lose my nerve if I did. I just ran as fast as I could off that high dive and was all business about what a great deal I found in 321Divorce. And how we could get this all done by Monday!

And the best part was that we didn't have to spend $7,000 on a lawyer, I said.

As long as you don't contest it. . . .

He surprised me by his calm. He seemed to see the logic and thriftiness in going the DIY route, and even though he said he didn't want the divorce, he may have been getting battle fatigued like me.

So our long weekend of DIY Divorce began. I brought my laptop over to our house and decided to go through the whole process there. I suggested he sit with me as I filled out all the forms so he wouldn't have to take the time to go through and second guess or dispute my work. I told him that I was determined to file by Monday so I could move into the new year with a clean slate, details and drama behind me. I was urgent not to spoil one more year of my life sparring with him.

He sat at the table with me from start to finish. It took us a few long sessions over a couple days to go through all the paperwork. Everything went pretty smoothly. We even took a break at one point and went out to eat and actually had a fairly enjoyable time. For the most part, we worked and played well with each other.

Until we didn't.

Reminding me again, why we were getting divorced.

We made it through the bulk of the paperwork with matter-of-fact ease. Until later in that second day, when we both got sucked into our familiar relationship 'round and 'round.

Luckily for us, as if divine intervention came upon us, we got a text from one of our tenants. We manage a few rental properties together and throughout this whole awful process, we have strangely been able to shift from battle to business on a dime. It was a simple thing that needed tending to but a perfect way to break up the demon dialogue[1] we were having.

While he was away, I moved along the process and was up to the financial forms. We both dreaded this part. All our financial stuff was going to come up and it could cause a lot of trouble, I feared. The agonizing detailed questions like how much do you make, how much do you spend on this or that, and other exhausting questions, picked at my patience and pain.

The forms were boiler plate and clearly establishing a means for spousal support. But even though we had been married for 32 years, and I as a stay at home mom was technically due, I knew we didn't have that kind of money to play with so I wasn't going to put that burden on my husband.

That wasn't important to me at the time so we blew past those questions.

I just wanted our assets fairly divided so we could move on peacefully. And thankfully, the majority of the paperwork was pretty simple, especially since minor kids weren't an is-

---

1. As referred to in John Gottman's book, The Seven Principles For Making Marriage Work, a demon dialogue is the downward spiraling negative talk couples fall into without awareness. Left unchecked this pattern repeats itself and can destroy a relationship. Gottman's research has shown how happily married couples are able to pivot out of these demon dialogues and repair.

sue. We didn't have to deal with any of the forms regarding custody and child support.

The quick break to deal with a tenant issue couldn't have come at a better time. He seemed in a better place in his head, as was I. We were ready to roll up our sleeves and get back to work.

But first, I asked, could you please go downstairs and get the printout? As he turned the corner to get the form I may have quickly downed a shot of Grey Goose.

Desperate times call for desperate measures.

Chapter 14

The Filing

I have checking disease. Not really, but it is a thing sometimes. It's not unusual for me to check a couple times to make sure I locked the door or "turned the iron off" before I leave the house. Filing for divorce was like that for me. I was so hyper focused on getting all the paperwork ready by Monday morning, checking and rechecking every form, bringing out the editor in me. Every t and i had to be crossed and dotted. The courthouse opened at 8 am so I wanted to be prepared and on their doorstep first thing.

That goalpost came into view somewhere around Saturday afternoon when I felt more confident with the process and understood the next steps. When I started the process online I blindly thought once you filled the forms out, you just hit submit and you were done. Nope. Not exactly. But not too far off.

These online divorce programs just help you fill out the paperwork which to me is really an amazing service. I don't know how lawyers do it, but if I were a lawyer I'd use one of these services. Lawyers and mediators provide counsel beyond the paperwork of course, but the busy work of generating the documents is required regardless. I considered just going to the county and picking up the forms, but I felt the "hand holding" of the document service was perfect for me. And in retrospect, it saved a lot of time because much of the information was repetitive and you only had to input it once through the app. The program has a database of the required forms for divorce for nearly all the municipalities across the land. It serves up questions to you, then smartly populates all the forms based on your data and location. Then you just download the forms and print them out. Easy peasy.

But I didn't trust it. First of all, being the checking-disease type, I worried that I wouldn't have every single form filled out correctly, or that I'd be missing a form or two, which the program did warn me about. And secondly, I knew so little about the divorce process, other than only ever hearing it was nightmare, so I couldn't believe all I had to do was basically drop the papers off at the courthouse and that would be that.

It wasn't quite that straight forward, but again, not too far off.

My stomach was a bundle of nerves that Sunday, the day before we filed. I spent way too much time methodically organizing our stacks of papers. Each of us had a different set of forms, so I was grateful that my husband was cooperative during this filing process. We were able to get it all together pretty quickly because we did it together. A testament to the good parts of our marriage. Which were many. I knew he didn't want this divorce any more than I did, making this whole process more awful. Unmarrying is for sure one of the most bipolar experiences a person has to go through. It's both excruciatingly painful, but it's strangely wrapped in hope. The hope of peace. The ending of a madness neither of us could surmount.

I called the county courthouse before I started the paperwork to figure out what I needed to do once I had the forms completed. I was stunned at the simplicity of the procedure, so much so that I asked way too many obvious questions. I'm sure the gal on the other end was rolling her eyes every time she had to say, "Yes, that's it!"

I had planned to take the paperwork in myself, but my husband insisted on coming with me. He said he was there when we got married, so he would be there for this. (He didn't say the D-word. I wondered if he felt as queasy about the word as I did.)

At first I cringed at the idea of him coming along, but the more I looked at the paperwork, and specifically the most important form in the stack, the more I liked the idea of him with me. One take-away I got from my chat with my mom's lawyer was that the Affidavit of Consent was the most important form for my husband to sign. Signing that form basically means he's agreeing to the divorce as filed; that he will not contest it. If I filed alone, he could have up to 90 days to contest it, keeping me in limbo that much longer until he signed it. It also meant that he would have to get the form notarized and delivered to courthouse himself. These were two key tasks I worried wouldn't be a priority for him without a considerable amount of nagging.

Plus, there were a couple dozen forms between the two of us that needed to be notarized as well, so it was looking a little more hairy in the details. Considering all that, I was very grateful that he chose to come with me.

More than anything, I wanted this whole process behind me. It had taken over my world. For the previous year and a half, I walked with an uncertainty and in a state of limbo that dragged me down. I just wanted it over with. Having him with me was unsettling and anxiety-filled, but I was so glad he came along. Even though I felt great stress with him beside me, in a strange way it validated my decision. I was facing this big move with no insulation. No outside counsel or technical support. If I were to get cold feet it would have been then, with him walking beside me down that aisle to divorce, tempting me to change my mind and turn back. But I was able to do it even still. I walked into that courthouse with no ambivalence. No second-guessing. No regrets.

Before I moved out, I committed to several new habits that I intuitively knew were needed for me to complete this marathon of that which I couldn't even say. Things like meditating, doing yoga, eliminating alcohol, and drawing something new on my iPad everyday were part of my healthy new routine.

One discipline that made the biggest difference in my well being was a commitment to a consistent take off and landing of my days. My first hour and last hour.[1]

How we start our day sets the energy for our whole day. Screw that up and you pay for it in some way. Our vibes follow us and co-create our futures by the decisions we make with our every moment. Clearer heads, clearer moments.

How we end our day sets us up for the solid sleep we need to tackle tomorrow. We're just dumber and clumsier without adequate sleep. And considering how easily stress can mess with my sleep, creating a domino effect of doom starting with a migraine, I knew that if I didn't get a handle on my nighttime routine, I'd never have the high octane needed to scale the days ahead.

By the time that all important Sunday night before filing rolled around, I was pretty solid in this First and Last Hour routine, doubling down on all the "things" recommended for a good night's sleep including the most difficult to master: no phone before drifting off to sleep.

This night before my scariest leap off the high dive warranted no less attention.

But still, I worried about not getting enough sleep and starting my new day with a tumble. I remembered the night

---

1. See My Toolbox chapter at the end of the book for my first and last hour routines. Hopefully you'll take away a little inspiration too!

before our wedding, tossing and turning, believing the only worry on my mind was how I would make it through the ceremony without losing my veil. Little did I realize then that losing my mind, not the veil on my head, was my real lurking concern. Ambivalence is a confusing place.

So this night, before walking down the aisle of unmatrimony, I gave my gremlins the side eye to stand down. Please, I thought, let me sleep.

To my surprise, whether it be from a solid nighttime ritual or from a resolved state of mind, I slept through the night and awoke surprisingly with the excitement of Christmas morning.

I found myself smiling at myself in the mirror as I got ready for the day. Even audibly giggling and asking myself out loud what in the world had come over me?! Why are you smiling? Why the giggles? Was it nerves and fear? Or was it joy?

I carried on. Drying my hair. Putting on my face. Getting dressed. The rumbling persisted. I decided it was pleasant. More than pleasant. It was thrilling.

And then something just clicked.

This feeling. This is what I should have felt on my wedding day, I thought. This unbridled excitement of Let's Get This Party Started should have been all over me on my wedding day.

It wasn't. Not even close. But it wasn't because I didn't love the man I was marrying. . . .

It was in these moments that Monday morning when I

decided I would never ever, ever, ever get married again unless I felt this same kind of excitement often and consistently. Not that I was even considering marrying again, but if I ever flew close to those flames again, I thought, I sure as heck better feel that same fire in my veins as I did that morning I was about to unmarry.

I told my husband I would meet him at the courthouse at 8 am. I didn't want him to ask to ride with me. Not that he would have. I guess I was just setting the boundaries ahead of time. But even just the idea of meeting him made me anxious. What if he didn't show up? Either way. Both felt icky.

As I was gathering my stuff to leave, I realized there was one form I hadn't printed out so I needed to go back to our house. That's ok, I thought. I have plenty of time since I got up at 5, my early morning routine locked in.

The house was quiet and dark when I arrived. The printer was in his room downstairs, so, I would wake him. I guess that's ok. He needed to get up anyway, and being anxious that he wouldn't, I figured this would be the perfect wake up call.

I wasn't sure what kind of person in him I was going to meet up with that morning. I knew his heart wasn't in this whole thing. My nerves were wired tight with worry about what he would or wouldn't do.

Inhale, exhale. Slowly and measured. Everything in my view was in hyper focus. I needed every bit of awareness I could muster to get through the next couple hours of practicalities.

This was the dress rehearsal to our unwedding ceremony. The first official step to our final divorce decree. The actual ceremony was the final hearing that wouldn't come for at least six weeks. At that point, all we'd have left to do was say our reverse "I do's" to the judge.

I got the printouts without incident, packed up my folder of forms and I headed out the door alone, telling my husband I'd see him soon.

Driving the short trip to the courthouse, I fumbled for my phone considering what music, podcast or book would calm my nerves. Ultimately I chose silence and drove in a meditative trance, erasing all thought from my head and focusing only on my driving. The turns, the stops, the acceleration. Freeing myself from any judgement, analysis or worry of what lay before me. This whole unmarrying process has forced me to become better at cancelling the chatter in my mind which has been huge in helping me manage the stress.

I waited in the foyer of the courthouse a short time before my husband arrived.

Standing at the end of the diving board, it was now my turn.

We walked to the reception desk. "We're here to file for divorce. Where do we go?" I asked.

That was one simple bounce up and off the board. Into the pool I went. I said the word. Out loud and in public.

We were directed to the second floor, turn left and it's the first door on your right.

We took to the elevator, standing awkwardly side by side. I shared an uneasy smile with another rider.

We were to take our paperwork to the family court office first so they could make sure we had all our forms prepared properly. Essentially it was where the teacher graded our work. I knew this was coming and it brought on the same anxiety as waiting for the results on a final exam in college. Sitting in the waiting area with a handful of people there for all different, but deeply personal reasons, I couldn't help but reflect in both sympathy and gratitude. My worries were nothing compared to some. . . .

Within about 30 minutes our papers were graded. We passed! I just needed to return with two very simple forms before the final hearing. We were given the green light to file. "Just go downstairs to the clerk of court," she's said. "They can notarize all your forms and you're good to go."

Yes! I thought, feeling a little more confidence as I made my way to the side of the pool. . . .

We took the stairs down to the first floor and as we briskly walked, I heard deep cleansing breaths coming from my husband. I was surprised. That was something I always did when trying to calm my nerves, and tried to teach him, though I never really saw him embrace. I was glad to see he did in this moment. I hope it helped him.

When we got to the clerk's office we were given a buzzer like you'd get at Applebee's and told to sit and wait. More time to sit awkwardly side by side, reflecting in more sympathy and gratitude for the problems we didn't have. If you ever need to bring yourself down to earth when you're all up in worry about your problems, just go sit in the clerk of court's office for twenty minutes.

Just when I was feeling awash in mental anguish, our buzzer blared and flashed. Our table was ready. We were walking down the aisle to publicly declare that our marriage was over. Once these papers were filed, the world would know. Which in both of our minds, wasn't a little bit of a thing. It was everything. Our shared identity for 32 years. The cornerstone of our family of six. Set to unravel at my own doing.

As we approached the clerk, I held my breath. What would he do? All the while in the courthouse that morning I held faith in the multiple sheriff's deputies that surrounded the place. Certainly they would protect me from him if he went berserker. Not that he would, but there have been times when his anger superseded his awareness in public.

He reached the counter one step before me. Before acknowledging the clerk behind the glass he turned to me and said in a tone that rang out like a boldface dare, but most certainly inaudibly for anyone but me, "Are you sure you want to do this?"

His last attempt to save us.

Without a word, I took my place beside him and pushed the stack of paper under the glass.

The clerk and I exchanged a glance lasting just long enough for me to know she knew. She knew exactly what I was going through.

She shuffled through the stack of papers, assessing and preparing them for our signatures. I held my breath some more.

I waited for the Affidavit of Consent.

I watched her slide it under the glass toward my husband. I wonder if she was aware of my screams inside?

He signed it. I exhaled.

Finally I felt relief. The rest of the papers were signed and stamped and processed without much of my notice. I confirmed that I would return with the remaining forms later that day. She said not to worry. I could do it on the day of the hearing. Nope, it would be done today, I said to myself.

Every t crossed. Every i dotted.

I returned later that day, got a beeper, and randomly got the same clerk from the dozen or so that were working. I handed her the papers. She recognized me from the few hours before. I asked her when our case would become public record. This was something my husband was extremely anxious about. I told him I would find out. Certainly even if it were today, unless someone was specifically searching for our name, it wasn't like it would be headline news on the county website. The clerk confirmed my thoughts and said, "You sure don't need one more thing to worry about today," she said with the bedside manner of someone who had been through the same.

Those few words of sympathy meant more to me in that moment than she could ever imagine. Nothing is random.

Throughout this whole ordeal of unmarrying, facing the stripping down of one's long-held identity stung the worst to me. You just can't predict the amount of time you'll need to really and fully accept this barenaked new you. Whoever that is.

As we walked out of the courthouse that day, papers filed, unmarrying in process, my husband reached for my hand.

My heart broke into a thousand pieces as I quickly pulled my hand away. No, I said. I can't.

We walked silently to our cars. He was parked a few rows away from me. As we turned the corner to walk down our row of parked cars, waffles popped into my mind. Should I?

"How about we go to Waffle House," I blurted out before I had time to think of the millions of reasons why not.

He looked at me like I was crazy. I've seen that look a million times before. I knew it meant yes.

I certainly didn't plan that I would file for divorce, then not only go out for breakfast with my soon-to-be ex husband, but spend the day with him as well. It wasn't in the book I never read about How To Get Divorced. It was just one more How that revealed itself and invited me to embrace. I may have been feeling exhilaration, but I knew it wasn't likewise for my husband. I couldn't let him walk away alone. Not this day.

We made it through the day with only a little bit of turbulence, but overall I believe sharing that time together laid a new, yet healthy foundation for a family that can never be broken.

It wasn't until the sun set that evening that I could understand why I was feeling so much strength and exhilaration on a day I assumed would be dark, depressing and raging in disappointment.

It was because of Hope.

More specifically, a certainty of hope. Now, it was up to me. And only me. No longer was I entwined to someone who pummeled that certainty with mistrust.

Hope equals potential. And even though the sum of my potential is lesser than with two, I can trust in the certainty of my one. If I didn't make it, it was of my own doing alone. I could accept that. And with no regrets. The dice was thrown.

Another leap was made.

Chapter 15

The Hearing

Sadness snuck up and flooded my face. Around 7 pm the night before our final divorce hearing, impending doom started its sneaky dance in my head. I had avoided thinking about the obvious throughout the days that preceded, busy slaying other gremlins while at the same time trying to stay steady. I knew I couldn't dig into what this hearing really meant. I'd never make it to the other side if I did.

But by that evening, my gremlin guard lay asleep, leaving me to see disappointment in the shade of every sorrow, grievance and dashed hope that brought me to this place.

I really didn't see this sadness coming. The day I filed, I felt such exhilaration. What happened to that, I wondered?

I knew I couldn't allow this despair to go unattended that evening. I sopped up the sadness and followed through with measured steps through my nighttime routine. Awareness called in, I knew I needed every bit of my head about me so I could sleep long and well, ready to face this no-turning-back dive to come.

Our hearing was scheduled at 9 am. I woke to my 5 am alarm, rested and thankful that I made it through the night.

I did my thing. Calmly and paying attention to every step. Yoga, meditation, shower, coffee, face, hair, dress. In times of stress, I've learned this is the best way for me to steer clear of a break down. Focus on the smallest of tasks with no judgement, no commentary, no thinking. No past. No future. Just now. Don't take your thoughts too seriously. I recently dashed this on the wall above my bathroom mirror. Better yet, have no thought at all. At a time like this, I knew the last place I needed to be was all up in my head.

I chose my outfit carefully. What do you wear to your unwedding? I picked a white buttoned down knit top and dark gray denim-like leggings. Wearing white seemed most appropriate. Although an ending, this was my beginning. I needed to keep in that spirit. I chose my sassy high healed ankle boots to keep reminding myself of that energy. Every time I looked down, New Maria was smiling back at me in those playful boots.

I took a selfie before I left. It seemed like the thing to do. A timely portrait of my unwedding. A face of heartbreak stared back at me.

I reflected for a second on how my previous trip to the courthouse felt completely opposite. Glee is not the word I would use to describe this morning.

I arrived in plenty of time to find the courtroom and settle into whatever was about to happen. All I had heard was that it would go quickly. Other than that, the courthouse carries its own special brand of terror that kept me in suspense. I'm not one for horror movies, so I did what I could to cover my eyes to this fright.

Since my husband had signed the Affidavit of Consent, he didn't need to be at the hearing, but he insisted. Certainly that added to my nerves. What would he do? What would he say? I've never seen him shy in a courtroom. Regrets of an unfollowed career in law hangs on him. I worried he would go all Perry Mason on me.

I found a seat against the wall outside our assigned courtroom. This was not a happy place. Except for the lawyers and bailiffs, pros who were impervious to the doom that loomed, the heaviness in that lobby could be seen on the faces of all the other amateurs like me. I crossed my legs and swung my foot nervously as I scrolled through my phone looking for any sort of distraction. My husband still hadn't arrived and it was 8:55 a.m. I rolled my eyes inside. So many fights we had with him insisting that I was ALWAYS late. . .

He arrived with only about a minute to spare. He strode in, addressed me with an energetic fake smile and sat down next to me, one seat apart. Almost nine o'clock, the tension between us was thick and awkward. Without a thought, I blurted out a decision about my business that hit me in the minutes before. It was one of those a-ha moments gravely misplaced again. Why I had to tell him then, I don't know. But it wasn't one of my better ideas. He rapidly fired a defensive retort. I volleyed back, regretting what I had just started. He retreated. I exhaled. The bailiff called us; we were part of a group of about 20 people sitting outside the courtroom who were ushered in for their moment to be heard.

This courtroom was specifically slated for family issues; divorce, adoption, name change, custody issues, etc. I filed into the middle row, my preferred seat in any setting. The procedure started quickly with an "All rise, raise your right hand," oath we were all to acknowledge. Within about 20 minutes a half dozen cases had already been heard. In between each case was the shuffle of paperwork as the judge signed off on one decree or request after another. This was a perfect preview to warm me up for what was to come.

Except for a name change and adoption case, all other parties were accompanied by their lawyers. But not this DIY girl.

Soon we were called. My husband ushered me through the half door from the gallery with a chivalry I have always appreciated. We stood side by side behind the lectern at this alter of our divide. In less time than it has taken me to write this paragraph, the deal was done. The judge asked each of us if we were in agreement with the settlement. We both replied, "Yes sir." Our reverse I do's had been said. The judge followed up granting me permission to change my name back to my maiden name and that was that.

We were officially unmarried.

The bailiff handed each of us a piece of paper that confirmed what just happened, and in a blink, we were walking back down the aisle as Not Husband and Wife.

To the edge of the pool and out, this time missing both an

m-r-s and that spring in my step that I had come to know from dives gone past.

My now ex husband opened the door for me as we left the courtroom. The second I walked through those doors, the spigot turned on, quickly beginning to seep through my eyes. Deep breath in. Deep breath out. Now it was me. I was coming unglued with every step.

He matched my sped up pace as we moved through the marble halls and out the door. We walked in silence the stretched-out distance to the parking garage next door. Up the three flights of stairs and around the corner to our row of cars; mine first, his beyond.

I started to open my car door when I felt him standing in wait. I turned, looked into his eyes and let open the flood gates. Big ugly tears rushed out. He asked if I wanted a hug. I embraced him, feeling comfort in his tight grip.

Abruptly I released his hold. Go Maria, I heard my screams inside. Go. You're done. You must let go. . . .

I reached for my door handle and looked back at him. He asked me if I was going to be alright.

I replied inaudibly and got in my car, hoping he'd stop me, but knowing he wouldn't. Rescuing me wasn't his style. When he was a wreck the day we filed, I stayed with him the whole time, starting with waffles. Now with me falling apart, and him standing tall, I found myself again sucked into expectations of comfort from a man who just would not.

From anyone else's back porch, this would seem like an

illogical expectation, but feelings don't care about facts. I was hurt all over again by a dashed hope for the one thing I've only ever wanted from him; his comfort and care.

I pulled out of the parking garage blinded by tears, knowing I did the right thing, but overwhelmed by a tidal wave I searched to define. I saw the girl that was me, shedding her pain, behind the wheel in the morning commute, drowning out who was really in charge. I was both aware and unaware of the storm that was barreling through me.

I fumbled for my phone and dialed my lifelong friend Katarina to share this moment with, sorrowful and all.

Two months before filing the paperwork, as I was winding my way through the business of divorce, I texted Katarina and told her I had something big to share, but needed to tell her in person. Not yet. But soon, I said.

I invited myself to her home across the country and told her I would fly out at some time in the next couple months. She comforted me with the love and trust we had shared for decades. Never pressuring me for details, she has been holding space for me throughout my life for both my millions of words, and now with my less than ten. And with that, our souls joined hands, connected with this simply worded text. I felt her support every step that followed even though she didn't know what I was going through. This dear old friend of mine was with me the first moment I laid eyes on this man

I didn't even know, but said I would marry. There was no question that she would be the first to know of its reverse.

We lived on opposite coasts, so I gathered up flight information and put ideas in my back pocket. I decided I would not go to see her until after I had either officially filed for divorce, or made significant-there's-no-turning-back progress. I couldn't bear talking about what ifs and what's next. I needed to be beyond that. I laser-focused on moving into my grand new year, free from the stench of years' past.

By the second week in January I boarded my flight. I stayed a long weekend. I shared my tears and fears, feeling an acceptance that has been the glue holding she and I close for more than 30 years.

Since I returned, she has been my rock. I can't imagine having faced this most treacherous high dive without Katarina. Keeping connected daily through the video messaging app Marco Polo, our friendship has deepened to a level beyond my imagination. We have filled each other's cup sharing both joys and sorrows and all in between like two little girls on a never ending sleepover.

A trusted soul to share life's highs and lows on a deeper level is essential to healing. I highly recommend this app for making up the miles. Like FaceTime without the urgency, video messages can be listened to and responded to in your own time. Visual yet without the pressure of a live phone call. You hear more deeply. And share more deeply.

As I pulled out onto the highway that morning after leaving the courthouse, Katarina was the only person this girl with the sorrowful tears wanted to call. A dear soul in my life who not only knows the depths of my heart, she knew my story. A story I couldn't speak out loud to anyone.

My words splashed out into a video river of salty drops. The shedding of a past life had begun. This is the first time I really felt the death of divorce.

With my first ugly cry of the day behind me, I headed to my mom's. One look at her and out came more rain.

"You've done a good job, Maria." I knew what she meant. This wasn't a comment of making a passing grade. It was the unconditional acceptance from my oldest sister-of-the-soul who knows from whence I came, and believes in where I can now soar, as only a mother can know.

"You did the right thing. If you didn't do it now, you would never do it," she said, adding that if I had waited even just five years, it would be too late, which brought me back to more math. I would be 60 years old . . . the longer I waited, the harder it would be to start all over.

"Now it's your turn, Maria," she said.

I decided to step away from the business of my life that day and go to the beach. There's no festive reception following an unwedding. I wasn't sure what to do. Running away for the day seemed like the best balm for me.

Living only about an hour from an uninhabited and often

desolate national seashore on the east coast of Florida, I had made a weekly routine of walking up and down this shoreline over the last several months. Hand-in-hand with every wicked emotion that followed me throughout this unmarrying journey, I chanted out loud my go-to mantra, "accept, detach, surrender" until my voice trailed off in exhaustion. These shores called in my angels. Somehow, after an hour or two of footprints in the sand, I drove home each time feeling renewed and stronger, if only for the day.

On this unprecedented day of my Unwedding, I needed to put into words this intensity of emotion I could not name. I had come too far and have jumped off too many high dives to not face whatever this storm was going on inside head on. I wanted a clean slate, and that would never happen if I stuffed this sorrow that screamed out for my care.

I interrupted the hour's drive of sobbing by stopping at Walmart to pick up beach chairs and an umbrella. I bought two chairs because you never know who might want to sit down beside this new free agent called Me. As I shut my car door to go into the store, I immediately felt the pang of Oh crap! I just locked my keys in the car. As if the gods knew I needed a break from my wailing, this easy to solve interruption actually did give me a much needed reprieve.

Door unlocked, I slipped back into my trance, completing the drive to my emotional oasis by the sea. I set up my brightly colored chair and matching umbrella firmly in the sand. This time I didn't walk. Not yet at least. I just cried. I sobbed. And sobbed. And sobbed some more. Flashes of memories spread out before me like a spastic slideshow of sorrows and joy. The most heartbreaking wrapped around the sweet family we made. So much good canceled out by too much bad. Over and over and over again. Until I realized its name.

These sobs were Grief. Ordinary and upsetting as you'd expect, teasing out unanswerables, drop by drop.

How could two good people have screwed up so badly? Two people who together faced years of piled on challenges and steep climbs in victory, yet now couldn't even solve a riddle of their own making?

I looked around at the few people that walked up and down the beach. I was alone. Lost in a world of others who clearly had it all figured out. Such a waste, I thought. This ending of ours.

With that, I walked. And walked. And walked. Accept, detach, surrender, I said firmly over and over until my throat screeched sorely to a halt.

After about 45 minutes I got distracted by a couple riding horses past me on that desolate beach. Bareback and blissfully in love, I turned around as if to follow their lead, watching as they disappeared along the horizon.

I deeply inhaled this change in scenery, allowing it to cleanse me with a new kind of wonder.

Step after step, I played with new thoughts, different ideas, and wild possibilities. By the time I returned to my spot in the sand, the lightness of Hope was sparkling through my eyes.

Something just clicked.

Time to go home.

Chapter 16

New Me

A rose is a rose is a rose is a rose.

Gertrude Stein

Gertrude Stein wrote in her 1913 poem, "Sacred Emily," that a rose is a rose is a rose is a rose. Kind of like our modern day way of saying, "It is what it is."

But there's more.

In Stein's view, this sentence expresses the fact that simply using the name of a thing already invokes the imagery and emotions associated with it.

Walking up the courthouse steps in 1987 to get our marriage license, I wasn't thinking about Gertrude Stein, or any rose by any name. Or about any other name but my own. The label of Me. Whoever She was.

It was time to declare what my name would become.

Other than being defined by from whence I came, a fresh new college graduate from suburbia Minnesota, I had no idea really who I was, or where I was headed. Except down the aisle in less than a week.

The last name that identified who I was up until that point, was expected to naturally be cast aside and in the end, rationalized as unimportant. And true, it probably was and still is.

Or is it?

I've wrestled with the significance of names for a good long time. From growing up with a slightly different version of a very popular last name, one that was commonly misspelled, mispronounced and made fun of, to a married name whose pronunciation immediately gave me a negative impression, I've had a knowing that the moniker we lead with indeed creates that imagery and emotion that Gertrude Stein was talking about.

Both of these were my given names. One given to me by my parents. One given to me by my husband.

They weren't me. But I became them. I adapted. I grew into them.

But mostly I set them aside, more insignificantly than they really were to me.

That day on the courthouse steps as a soon-to-be bride I knew how it would all end. I just got there kicking and screaming. In silence.

Back in the 80s, the feminist movement was in full force. Women were sold the idea that we could have it all, do it all, AND fry it up in a pan. The Enjoli perfume commercial from 1980 fooled a generation of women into believing they can and should do it all. "...bring home the bacon, fry it up in a pan, and never ever let you forget you're a man...." All with their 8 hour perfume.

Did anyone ever do the math on that?! That's a lot to do in eight hours.

By the time I was faced with changing my name, the world was all about hyphenation under the guise of feminine power. Ultimately, it seemed to me to be a pompous way of being one foot in and one foot out of marriage. What were we trying to say? That we kinda wanna be connected to this man, but kinda don't? After all, he doesn't have to give up his name, we all reasoned with our best second grade logic. If he doesn't have to, why do I?

But then the complications pile on. What about the kids? What will they be called? How do you fill out those forms? What about your given middle name? Does that go away? Or do you just have a really long name that doesn't fit on any form?

I went to the courthouse that day with my sister and my mom. My mom patiently waited me out as I wrestled with a pen and the simple form. My sister however had little patience and ordered me in her typical bossy way to just fill it out and put down my soon-to-be husband's name.

I didn't really say much at all. I stewed and stirred inside, and finally decided to keep it simple and take my husband's name. Not because my sister said so, but because it was logical.

And after all, what's in a name anyway? It's not me.

It just labels me.

This is where things get complicated. Not just for me. But for all ya'lls.

Our journeys through life pile on one thing after another. Good, bad and indifferent. Our names become so secondary, they're like our car keys. We don't even notice them anymore. We grab them and go, using them pretty much everyday, but we don't give them too much significance.

Until we lose them.

Or get a new car.

Suddenly they're the only thing that matters. It gets really personal. If we dig a little deeper we realize we're connected to something that displays who we think we are. Like our bodies, our hairstyle, our clothing, etc.

Pants don't make the man. The man makes the pants.

But does he?

We could volley around that idea to infinity and never feel satisfied. Like a dog chasing his tail, there is no end.

Until we can see the separateness.

The pants. The man.

The name. The girl.

The ego. The essence.

It matters. It doesn't.

By the time I reached the courthouse steps three decades later at the ceremony of my unwedding, my name, which had come to define ME, became all boogered-up in a stew of family, children, business and community. The rose was the rose was the rose was the rose. She is what she is.

But with a swift stroke of a pen, all that would unravel. That Me would soon not be. Suddenly terror flooded me at the thought of being asked an innocent question like, "How's the family?"

I would no longer be the She I came to believe I was. A happily married woman. With a beautiful family. Living a sweet lifestyle. In my dream home. On a pretty little street in a pretty little town. Who for years could answer that question easily. The family is great!

The reality was we weren't great. The family was shaken and torn. I felt like a failure. Wrought with shame and gut punching guilt. A girl who consciously dismantled her dream to save the She that resided in Me.

Who did she think She was? I didn't know, but now I could find out.

Identity crisis day one.

What followed our final inking, the unraveling of he and me, was my final trip off the high dive of divorce. A leap that seems like it would be just a footnote, lurked and terrorized me with every single step.

The coming out. The public reveal. The no-turning-back, indelibly written and cancelled out She that had become Me after three decades of piled on A equals B.

Where did she go? Time to let them know.

Climbing up for one more splash.

No one but our kids, my mom and my friend Katarina knew of our divorce when it was all going down. (Well, my hairstylist knew. But that goes without saying, right?) Now that we were officially unmarried, I needed to move forward with this new life I had hoped to find. But the reality of walking down the street and being met with a simple how are you, how's the family seemed terrifying if I didn't make it clear as to who I wasn't anymore.

The last thing I wanted to do was talk about it. To anyone. Too much shame, pain and unbearable hurt. I knew though, that in order for light to come in, I had to let the darkness out. It was time to throw open the doors and let people in.

As much as I didn't want to reveal my story, I knew avoiding it and letting gossip lead the way was worse. You can't avoid being the subject of gossip when it comes to divorce, but when you lead with your authenticity, people hear your heart and you nurture your broken soul.

So we started with his mother. I logically reasoned that she needed to hear the news from him, not from me, and certainly not through the social grapevine that was soon to be in full bloom.

My not-anymore husband agreed to make the call with what I'm sure was great dread. A high dive moment for him no doubt. He didn't have a very close relationship with his mother. She didn't know of any of our unravelling as far as I knew. She would be blindsided by this news for sure. I imagine it was one of the hardest calls he's ever made. Sadly, I don't think her short and sterile response was very comforting to him though. I felt really bad for him. And me. Injured Little Me assumed she celebrated this news. Not of her son's pain but of the departure of me. I don't think she held much fondness towards me.

After that, it was my turn. I needed to tell my siblings and closest friends. I would've preferred to just text them, but I felt this kind of news was a little more significant and really warranted a call, which I dreaded for all the reasons above. I just didn't want to talk about it.

Thankfully, Marco Polo came to mind. I could express what I needed to say while hiding my shame behind the lens of this video messaging app. Another high dive for me. I brushed my hair, gathered up my courage and jumped. I rattled off one personal message after another. Each one surprisingly easier to express, even though I danced around the icky word and said we "split up" rather than divorced.

Now with that done, it was time to face the public square. Again, technology was on my side. With one fell swoop, I could let the world know my new status with little more than a click.

Facebook's change of relationship status could do that in an instant.

But icky. I couldn't. As easy as that seemed, it certainly

would bring about all sorts of gossip and questions that I didn't want to deal with. I needed to brave my way up the diving board again, create my divorce announcement in the same vein as one would announce an engagement. Or marriage. Or birth.

It was a birth after all.

It was the birth of a New Me.

I had never seen a Divorce Announcement so I was in uncharted waters. It's no wonder. Divorce is a cringy thing to announce. 'Cuz shame. And so much more.

But it needn't be. When you step aside from your gremlins tearing yourself apart with guilt and shame, you realize divorce is just one more step in our timeline of life. We need to stand up and honor that.

So I did what I knew I could do. I could write. From the heart. And just let it go.

I decided to create a whole new Facebook account. I didn't want to delete the account I had for the last decade, full of sweet memories of my family. My life. My old Me. But I knew I had to start fresh. From a clean slate. For New Me.

I put my old account on ice and started a new one with my new name. A single post, and a couple of my closest friends. I didn't want to search and invite the hundreds of friends and acquaintances I had accumulated over the last decade on Facebook. I figured the bots would bring them to me and they'd knock on my door if they wanted to know New Me.

In a very short time, my notifications were buzzing from

so many friends who discovered New Me and who piled on compassion and filled my heart with love. That's the true beauty of social media. Connections. And what we all need. Regardless of how the darkness makes us say we don't.

Two years later, my identity crisis continues to pester me, but it definitely has waned in its power over me. I have officially changed my name. But with a twist. I brought back my maiden name but also changed my middle name. I figured if I was going through all the literal hassle of changing my name, I might as well anoint it with new meaning. Meaning that for me, is more significant than just because my parents liked the sound of my old one. So I pushed the envelope. I colored outside the lines and took on my Grandmother's first name as my new middle name. A woman of strength and sass who lived by the beat of her own drum. Plus I liked the sound of it.

A name given to Me. From Me.

Soon came a new social security card, new license and new passport. The first three of a dizzying number of administrative changes that will probably take a lifetime to edit but are shaping this New Me.

I've faced identity like never before throughout this whole unmarrying process. The biggest thing I've learned is that the Me that resides inside has never changed. There's nothing New about Me. I am the same Me I was before I came into this world. And the same Me that will leave this world.

The challenge we all have is when we get our Me all tangled up in What We Think Is Me.

A diminished sort of Me results.

A rose is a rose is a rose is a rose.

Same same, same same it is not.

Chapter 17

First Facebook Post

No one ever talks about how to announce your divorce. Or even if you should. The whole shaming experience of divorce puts you in a crawl-under-the-covers mood for a really long time. The last thing you want to do is make some big announcement. But if you don't, the world you orbit will eventually figure it out and you'll walk around with that weird elephant in the room dodging queasy looks on people's faces who don't know what to say to you. That's where Facebook is really handy. In one post I could release all I had been carrying around into the fresh air and start a new story. My load would lighten.

This is the first post in my new Facebook account for New Me. I was blown away with the love, support and encouragement I received. Facebook is best for things like this.

Dear Friends...

I'm coming out on the other side of where my WE has turned into a ME. Max and I have decided to split after 32 years of marriage. This change has been years in the making and not without an excruciating amount of thought and struggle. Although I am still raw and processing all that this means, I believe this was the right decision for our growth.

I will always truly love and respect Max and deeply appreciate all the experiences we've shared together, both the challenging and the joyful. We have sewn together a rich tapestry of a life story that has made us who we are today, and will be part of who we will become tomorrow. I am confident that each of our individual journeys will offer opportunities for growth that will continue to add more depth to our lives, and for our family, going forward.

I want you to know that I appreciate all the love and support you have given us as a couple through the years. Although we may be separate now, that doesn't take away from the relationship we share with you as individuals.

Much love,
Maria

Chapter 18

Letting Go

This is the letter I wrote to my ex husband two years after our divorce. I chose to send him a letter in the mail because we weren't talking, at his request. I felt the need to provide some closure while at the same time clear the air for the undeniable lifelong connection we share through our four kids. An email seemed too sterile.

Dear Max,

It's been so many years, I can't do the math in my head anymore. We've spent more years intimately by each other's side than not. Depending on our longevity, we'll both be hard pressed to find anyone to match those numbers for either of us in this lifetime.

But you and I together were more than just a timeline or pile of years. We started from scratch; a tiny spark that dashed across a crowded room. Together we fired up the stuff that made a lot of amazing. A livelihood, a lifestyle, and most importantly, a family.

I can't say I never saw it coming. Our great unraveling. But I certainly never wanted it. Now two years out, I see we really had no other option. I was stuck. You were stuck. We were in an endless do-loop of destruction that kept each of us in a misery that had no escape.

But confusing to me amidst all the hard times was that there were a lot of good times. They just couldn't compete with the bad in those final years. So now for me, two years post divorce, and with a lot of healing, the good is starting to come into vibrant focus and is cancelling out all of the bad. And I'm so grateful for that. Grateful for you, and all that we came to be together.

Max, I see so many of the mistakes I made in our marriage with so much more clarity than ever. I hurt you in so many ways. There was so much I didn't understand within myself and how to express that to you that I lashed out and made life confusing for you at best, and torturous at worst. And from that, I've carried around guilt and shame like a couple of worn out blankies perpetuating a suffering in me that only created more suffering for you.

These last couple years I've hosted hundreds of "if onlys" in my mind. Disappointments equally distributed between the two of us, making me finally realize we really knew not what we did. Rattling around in my head were all kinds of ways to say, "If only we had more how-to, awareness and etc., we might still be together."

But lost in that hamster wheel of thought is the actual fact that we didn't know. We hadn't grown. And we were so stopped-up in the works that we couldn't grow.

It's like saying I wish my six year old self could swim as fast as my 16 year old self. It couldn't happen without growth.

I acknowledge my wrongs and I understand "us" more than ever. What's happened over all those years, and where it's taken us both in challenge and in joy. I see you. With compassion and clarity. And surrender the pain I've been carrying around that's wrapped up in you.

It's my hope that one day we can be friends in celebration of one another rather than in avoidance. Avoidance of that final frontier of each of us moving on and finding a new someone that will fill our final years.

To that end, I have been exploring the dating world and have not been surprised to find both exhilaration and frustration. The newness masks the demons all of us carry forward and beg us for just as much care as ever before. Over time, I have found someone who sees me wholeheartedly, yielding to my demons and dreams alike. I can't predict the future, as relationships are tricky at best, but for today, I have peace. I wish that for you as well.

I want you to know that I appreciate all that we had together and look forward to a day when we both can release all the bad and appreciate all the good that shines in the faces of those four beautiful people we have made. We will always be a family. Regardless.

Much love,
Maria

Chapter 19

Sidelines & The Lost Chapter

In a quirky twist, I'm writing this chapter right before I publish this book, three years after my divorce. (I can finally say the D word.)

Just when I think all my high dives to unmarrying are done, I faced another one yesterday. For the last several months I've been working on my final edits and formatting this book. I stayed away from posting anything on social media as I went through the process. I've been very measured in my process, taking my time, dotting all my i's and crossing all my t's. My goal was to publish my book by the end of the summer.

So the other day, nearing my deadline at the end of August, I jumped in and made a video for my Instagram announcing my soon-to-be-released book *UnMarrying My Best Friend.*

But that wasn't just that.

I've been putting off this reveal for weeks. Methodical in my process as I was, dragging it out is probably more descriptive. I twisted myself into my own catch-22. As much as I wanted to help others with my story, I would have to literally share my story. That was the big step I dreaded the most.

Because fear. Fear that the last bits of who I was would now be wide open and on display. Then poof! Gone with one declaration. The last person I wanted to see this revealing was my ex husband. Because why? Identity. The final no-turning back, let-go detaching of who I was combined with all the things that make us feel insecure about who we are becoming.

You may have confidence in your chosen path, but until you say it, it's not really real.

That's the moment your knees start to shake and you get unsteady. It's a riddle of uncertainty that can't be avoided with growth and change.

That's when I realized I was once again climbing another high dive. Even with all the bounces off that board before, I was surprised at the gremlins still harassing me inside. But I knew if I didn't make this last leap into New Me, my journey would not be complete.

I realized if I put off sharing this story, life would roll on without me while I clung tightly to the sidelines, married to my fear of letting go. And this burning-inside-me purpose to help others face their scariest life changes would cower into a nothingness from over-rated Who Do You Think You Are-ness.

And then I remembered I had been here before. . . .

Remember when I told you I didn't confide in anyone about my unmarrying except for my mom and hair stylist? I realized I left out someone really important. For reasons I now remember why. I wanted the focus of this book to not be on the heart-wrenching pain I felt every step of the way, but rather the big steps that are crucial to unmarrying and how I made it through them. Less about my pain and more about the process.

But after I publicly shared and declared this upcoming new book, I felt a deja vu from a time before I even made my final decision to d-i-v-o-r-c-e.

That feeling of watching the world from afar. Separate and disconnected from a movie you're not even part of.

Back to my journal I went. What happened back then?

Scrolling back through my posts I found it. The day I told my sister.

It was the weekend before Thanksgiving. I found myself sitting on a park bench in the middle of our sweet little downtown, watching all the passerby's. I'm pretty sure I was clinically depressed looking back on it. Carrying around a persistent lump in my throat and watery eyes, the sunny Florida day did all it could to brighten my spirits but to no avail. I watched families stroll by, smiling and chatting. Couples walking hand-in-hand giggling and cooing. I pinched back my blubbering sorrows, making me more and more agitated.

Until something just clicked. I realized I was watching the world go by, like someone else's Hallmark movie, while I wasted away on the bench. Sidelined by my own choosing.

I knew that if I didn't face this and start sharing my story and bringing it to a reality, I would be in this uncomfortable and degenerative limbo forever. . . . I would never feel the love and joy that those people walking by must be feeling, heart to heart, hand-in-hand. Either I jump and get divorced or I turn back. I can do either one.

But I don't want to turn back, I said in my journal.

I just don't feel like it's the right thing for me to do so I must go forward and start facing it. And I need to do it before the holidays so I don't have to fake my way through it. I'm trying to be as authentic as I can be. I want to live in truth from now on. I don't want to hide behind a façade anymore. And the only way I can do that is to start facing this by telling a close family member and being real.

This journal entry continued to reveal the beginning of my journey to New Me, unbeknownst to me at the time.

I hesitated so much in reaching out to my sister but something kept pushing me so I went with my gut and texted her before I lost my nerve. I invited her downtown for dinner. She suggested that I come to her house as she just lit a fire in her fireplace, but I just couldn't.

I felt the need to be in a neutral place. Being at her house would make me feel even worse and more like a loser. I don't know why exactly but probably because I compared my messed up life with her perfect looking life. She's maintained her family so well; what's my problem? I know it's not rational but fears generally aren't.

She soon met me downtown for dinner. We talked about her family and other general things and then she asked me how I was doing. . . .

After a very long and uncomfortable pause I let it out. It was so hard to say the words. I knew once I said it, it would be real. But I also knew I could turn around and get off the diving board and not say a thing about what was really happening. . . .Somehow I blurted it out. I told her I moved over to Mom's . . . . There was no turning back now. Shame and grief poured out.

I am proud of myself for actually doing it. But now I feel raw. And totally lost.

She was really good about it. For all my fears, I was surprised at her compassion toward my shame. She said no one thinks about what you're going through like you do. We both teared up and exchanged stories and I felt her genuine care for me. She said she would be there for whatever I needed. I am so thankful for my big sister. <3

By the end of the evening I was a wreck. As I drove home I could only feel one thing....and it came pouring out my eyes....

Who am I now?

What I've learned about major life change is that it's not a one-and-done thing. It's a process. Evolving and growing into a New You is more than a name change or status unwound. It's a journey that keeps serving you more opportunities to lace up your shoes and find your balance. Until finally one day you decide to step away from the sidelines and into a whole new game. Batter up!

Afterword

Three years later . . .

This morning I stumbled on a text I received from my husband more than three years ago, dated just weeks before I moved out. About nine months before the divorce.

It was heartfelt and apologetic. He was trying. He took ownership for the hurt he caused me and he was reading the book I suggested he read. He wanted to talk to me about ways to improve our emotional connection.

My heart stopped. I immediately wondered if I had seen it. How could I have left him if I had?

That's the trickery of printed words without a full face feel.

On the face of it, his text seemed to answer all my needs. It seemed authentic and humble. Words that logically should create a better ending.

But as with all things, context is king. How I feel about those words today, three years later, now more healed and fulfilled, is completely different than what I was feeling then.

I dug back into my journal. I rarely look back at my journal entries but this time, I really needed context. I needed to get a feel for what was happening to me that very day. Who was that girl back then? And what was seeping through her eyes?

Reading through my journal entry of that day, and those that preceded and followed, helped me fill in the blanks and empathize with that girl from years past.

She is world's apart from the girl writing this last chapter three years hence.

She was a girl broken and torn. Untrusting and bedraggled. A girl who knew actions spoke louder than words and with a gut screaming that his rarely did.

She was a girl facing the unthinkable. A risky decision with only two daunting options. Each guaranteeing crushing pain to process.

One gambled on him.

The other gambled on her.

Would he really change? Or could she find a peaceful life on her own?

I will never know whether giving him one more chance, one more month, or one more year would have yielded the deep intimate connection I craved or not. But I do know where I am today. Living a peaceful life. Happy. And fulfilled.

Three years ago, the gamble on myself seemed like a long shot because I had such little value in myself. It seemed like the riskiest move but turned out to be a winning choice.

When facing the unthinkable, always remember, you can't change anyone else. You can only change yourself.

Throw the dice on you. Whatever that looks like. If you

stay in your marriage. Or not. You will always win if you bet on yourself.

Promise.

Unmarrying is more than a solitary event. It's a process. Just as it takes time for a marriage to transform us into the sum of two becoming one, so too does the division of unmarrying. It's a detaching from the identity of a union of mismatched intentions. An imperfect fraction wreaking in pain. The day of the divorce is the first big wack at that divide. The healing in the years to follow cuts away the tiny tendrils that bound you together until soon this union can be divisible no more. Healing is complete. Yet scars remain and remind.

The speed of healing is as unique as the couple themselves and impossible to predict. At three years out, I'm getting there. . . .

The last several years of facing my pain and fears and allowing them to roll through me has been the best Rx ever. It has opened up a channel of reflection and an expansion into a world of possibilities I would have never seen in Pretendyland. Most importantly it's shown me that I can not only survive, but thrive.

Sometimes (usually) things get worse before they get better. Just keep facing the things that scare you most.

Peace and love to anyone in this place of healing. This too shall pass. <3

Marriage is not an Entitlement Program

New Book Coming!

Years before I even considered unmarrying, let alone writing a book about it, I came up with the title of my next book.

Marriage Is Not An Entitlement Program.

Just because you're married doesn't entitle you to be a jerk. A snot. A brat. To be unkind. Prideful, uncompromising, stagnant, unkempt, lazy and impatient. The list goes on.

We all do it. Have done it. And will do it again.

Unless we become aware.

We have no idea that the errors of our ways are leading us to our bitter end some day. Whether that results in a full-on divorce or decades wasted going through the motions, unmarrying begins with the first eye roll.

It's a harsh reality I wish I understood before I said I do.

But this is the stuff no one tells us in the beginning. Then life piles on and we get all caught up in the details of he said she said.

No one wants to tell that doe-eyed dreamy couple any of this because we all know they probably wouldn't listen anyway. And what would we tell them? We were all that couple.

Sucked into the fantasy. The happily ever after. The security of Forever and the It Will Get Better.

The fine print is no more acknowledged than the terms and conditions we all skip through with every online enrollment.

Marriage is hard work, believed no one ever.

Modern day couples cross the threshold no differently than newly marrieds from decades past. Other than holding a PHd in Pinterest party planning, modern day couples are just as want of relationship skills as we were back in the day.

Unfortunately, the security that draws us into marriage is the very thing that kills it. We're so secure, we fall asleep on our own watch.

But it doesn't have to be that way.

In my own matrimonial unravelling and years since, I've discovered the very thing that makes certain our blissful demise. Hidden in the wide open, it's the couple slaying virus of Marriage Entitlement. ME for short.

Left untreated ME always leads to the reverse I do's. Your pairing could experience a short lived bout ending with a swift kick in the pants goodbye, or you could get taken to the grave with a life long case ending in death by a thousand cuts.

The good news is that it's preventable. Once you know the signs, you can start the cure.

ME is a sneaky little bugger though. Most people have it but have no idea. Never underestimate its power. It lurks in the background, symptomless (sometimes for years), lead by its nasty little leader Complacency. You may think that snarky little comment you said to him was harmless, or forgetting to take her on a date (last week, last month or all year) wasn't a big deal, but vibes don't lie. The words and circumstances may be forgotten, but count on disappearing passion with every tiny slight. Complacency clouds our memory of the sacred contract we made with each other under the stars, then sealed with a kiss the day we said I do.

This book is all about the reciprocity of relationship.

In the downward spiral of a marriage, the mind is fertile with reflection. Comparing and contrasting What Is with What You Want To Be. Constantly struggling to figure out the best way to find peace in a situation that's half out of your control. You realize over and over again, with each failed attempt, that you can't change another person. Try as you might, you can't do both sides of a relationship.

You can't be the pursuer and the pursued.

The feminine and the masculine.

The yin and the yang.

By definition that's not relating.

In one of my manic moments of frustration with my husband, the feeling of entitlement came blazing through my mind. As in, He Isn't Entitled To Treat Me This Way . . . just because we have this 'Til You Die contract.

And then I got a little more pissy. And creative.

Trade imbalances have a way of righting themselves. Either

with a new deal or parted ways. Imbalance is unsustainable.

First comes love, then marriage, then . . . more love or more pain. It's either one or the other.

This book will help newly marrieds, never marrieds and forever marrieds get back to the day when they weren't so familiar with each other. When they yielded and forgave. When they inspired and gave.

Without acknowledgment of our own undoing, and awareness of its signals, we are doomed. Long term relationships can't thrive on twinkies. We need to constantly nourish the souls of our other like our life depended on it. Because it does.

Loneliness is the leading cause of death. And just because you're married doesn't mean you're not lonely.

Remember seeing that old couple in the restaurant sitting across the table from one another eating in silence? We've all seen them. They may have sat down together but they are no where near each other.

If we're going to get outta here alive, we better start feeding each others souls like we did in our doe-ey eyed days gone by.

Blissfully fulfilling marriages don't just happen any more than really great kids. When we were raising our kids people always told to me that I was lucky to have such amazing kids. Yes they are and were amazing. But luck had nothing to do with it. They didn't just pop out that way. It took a lot of work. A tough job that my husband and I were really good at nurturing. And without a doubt my most fulfilling job ever.

If only we had given our marriage that much care. . . .
Instead we perished from a bad case of ME.

Marriage Is Not An Entitlement Program promises to be a page turner of both inspiration and strategy to grow a better You and Thee. It will help you spot the signs of ME in in your relationships and offer tips and tools to wind your way out of a certain demise if you don't do something soon.

Like it or not, although unmarrying is riddled in shame, it only takes one half of your pair, powered by enough pain, to quickly figure out getting a divorce is as easy as googling $99 Divorce.

Don't be blindsided. Going through divorce is way worse than the cure for ME.

With a pinky promise to the process and an Rx of Humble Pie, you and your honey will be well on your way back to those dreamy starry nights of days gone by.

If you want to be the first to see all my new books, sign up for my Launch Team. It's a blast. Not only will you be the first to read and review my books, but you will have access to exclusive content and bonuses as well as be part of a growing community of likeminded people who share the passion of Always Getting Better. Better people make the world a better place and that's just too amazing to pass up!

Go to www.somethingjustclicked.com/books

My Toolbox

Conquering Major Life Change With Grace

I wouldn't have made it through my divorce without access to the amazing resources I discovered along the way. It's wild how expansive our lives can be if we just dig in and open up our minds to figure things out. Divorce is a very solitary process. I found that the greater the inputs from sources outside my familiar world, the greater the courage. Inputs meaning new knowledge, ideas and perspectives. Repeating the same thing over and over in my head, or massaging the same sorrows with friends and family wasn't going to work. It wouldn't challenge growth. Plus I would drive myself and everyone else crazy.

An exception to this is if you are blessed with a friend who can bravely and lovingly tell you what you don't want to hear. If you have that kind of friend you have a true gift. But still keep expanding. That's where these tools came in. Through research and self discovery, I was able to patch together the courage to do the hard things I needed to do. The high dives were not going to disappear without me taking a bunch of leaps.

These are just some of the the books, tools and strategies

that have helped me. Go to SomethingJustClicked.com to find my always growing and updated list.

BOOKS

The Power of Now, Eckhart Tolle

The New Earth, Eckhart Tolle

These two books have been on my shelf for nearly 20 years. I raised my kids with principles presented in both of these books. These books will open your eyes to our clever and destructive ego and the relevance of time. By the time my marriage was facing its darkest days, I knew these books contained the foundational pieces that both my husband and I needed to master if we were going to survive. Clearly we didn't master them. But that is not a reflection on the quality of the message. I continue to be a student of the ego, a little monster I call my gremlin, and appreciate books like these that remind me again and again who's derailing my progress. Must have books for anyone in a relationship with another human, including one's own self.

The Seven Principles for Making Marriage Work: A Practical Guide from the Country's Foremost Relationship Expert, John Gottman PhD, Nan Silver

This is a book I got my hands on a little too late for my marriage. I believe my therapist recommended the works of John Gottman, but I really can't remember. Suffice it to say by the time I braved my way into therapy, my husband and I were so deeply wrecked, I could hardly open this book. I actually looked at it with disdain, so that tells you where I was then. I never abandoned the book though. I knew when I found the perfect man for me, who aligned with my intentions and accepted me wholeheartedly, that even we could use some guidance in relationship skills. I'm glad I kept it on my shelf. Its well worn pages are a testament to its brilliance. Get this book now. Your relationship needs it.

Too Good to Leave, Too Bad to Stay: A Step-by-Step Guide to Help You Decide Whether to Stay In or Get Out of Your Relationship, Mira Kirshenbaum
This is another book I discovered too late in the process. It would have saved me from a lot of mental gymnastics and confusion. It's like that very blunt, but loving best friend who can help you sort through an impossible decision. The biggest a-ha for me was you can't pro and con your way to a decision and that it's possible to lock yourself into the prison of ambivalence for the rest of your life. That meh feeling riddled in fear of the unknown that can easily seal your fate for a lifetime of unfulfillment is a decision we make every single day we choose to do nothing. This book puts the mirror in front of your face. Now you know. . . .

The Willpower Instinct: How Self-Control Works, Why It Matters, and What You Can Do to Get More

of It, Kelly McGonigal
This book was another life changer for me. All those years my mom told me to meditate and I just bobbled my head. Meditation . . . . whose got time for that?? Boy oh boy did this book change my mind. All it took was for her to say that meditation changes your brain. As in literally. It builds up the prefrontal cortex of our brain. The part in charge of all our rational decision making and discipline. What?! I'll have some of that please! Thank you very much.

Notes From the Universe, by Mike Dooley
This feel good book overflows with quirky and uplifting messages from a greater power beyond. Call that power what you want, but Dooley calls it the Universe. When you're going through a major life change or even just a regular day, these notes set you in a bold new direction you may not have considered. I've been a subscriber of his daily email *Notes* since before he even appeared in *The Secret* years ago. His musings have been powerful little reminders on how effortlessly life really can be.

Daring Greatly, by Brené Brown, PH.D., LMSW
This book came into my view at the perfect time. Just when I was frozen in fear and riddled in crushing shame and guilt at the very idea of divorcing. It opened my eyes to the idea that vulnerability is our greatest super power and that embracing the scary (or taking a leap off the high dive) is not nearly as

risky or as painful as playing it safe on the sidelines forever wondering what it would've been like had you jumped. A must read for helping you understand how guilt, shame and humiliation play a role in our lives both personally and culturally. You will see how showing your vulnerability not only is the most courageous thing you can do, but it is the only way you can be your most authentic self.

TOOLS

3StepDivorce.com

This is the document generating service I used. It's currently about $299 which is a fraction of the average cost of $11K per spouse if you went through a divorce lawyer. If you're able to reconcile the financials and don't have kids in the equation, I highly recommend this route. You're going to have to answer all these questions on these forms anyway, even with a lawyer. A lawyer, like a therapist, can't make the decisions. That's your work to do and you can't escape it with a pricey divorce lawyer. You also can simply go to the county where you're divorcing and pick up all the paperwork for free. But I found the ease of this service populating repetitive fields on the forms to be well worth the price.

Marco Polo

This is one of my favorite apps. I use it everyday. It's a video messaging app allowing you to share and reply in your "own time" versus in "real time." Have you ever gotten a call from a friend and didn't answer even though you love talking to them because you were in the middle of something or even just not in the mood to talk? Marco Polo provides the comfort of sharing when it works for you.

Plus as a one way messaging app, you can monologue your thoughts at an uninterrupted pace. Your rants and vents take on a life of their own without the pressure of a two way conversation. That alone is cathartic in a real talk-therapy sort of way. I'm not saying two way conversations aren't amazing too—I FaceTime everyday as well—but overall, Marco Polo is a comfortable place for growing a deeper bond with even your closest of soul connections when schedules and distance are an obstacle. More is shared. More is heard. Without the pressure of time.

This is yet again one more technology that is helping our species stay connected in ways never experienced even just a decade ago. This app showed me yet again how true connection is more than skin deep and needn't be sacrificed by time or miles.

Day One

This is the journaling app I have used for years. As of this writing, I've used it for 3,629 days in a row. A streak I can't seem to break! Holy Cow! That's 9.94 years. I've never done the math on that 'til now.

I committed to 30 days of journaling when I started and

was hooked. My rule was to simply write a sentence or two summarizing the day. It quickly turned into much more than that when I discovered I could dictate my journal entries. That made writing on the fly so much easier.

The app is accessible on mobile and desktop platforms. It's free but well worth the premium fee of about $3/month for added features like video, audio, Instagram importing, book printing and more.

I love the tagging feature which allows you to track significant times in your life such as moments with your kids, holidays, and as mentioned before, relationship issues. By being able to quantify how many fights we had within a certain period of time I was able to see the reality of the problem. It was staring me in face with a snotty I Told You So look. I was also able to easily find these entries to reflect on patterns of behavior. I don't think I can over emphasize the value of daily journaling for overall well being. Choose your method, but the processing of emotions in a safe, secure, password protected environment is Star Trek Land with Day One app compared to paper journals. Unless it's like the gold-key secured Holly Hobbie diary I had in fourth grade. :)

STRATEGIES

First Hour / Last Hour

My First and Last Hour routine helped me develop the clarity I needed to do the hard things unmarrying requires.

Intentionality with these two hours of the day moves you from basic surviving to thriving. If you do nothing else today, pay attention to your first and last hours. I promise you'll feel and function better. Figure out what gives you peace and permission to step away from your mind for awhile. Then make a deal with yourself. Do these things before going bed and when getting up. Only you can keep the peace in your head and you're gonna need a lot of it when facing your major life change or any challenging dream.

My first hour consisted of a shower, yoga and 20 minutes of mediation. Coffee was my incentive. If I did these three things I could have my coffee. It worked like a charm. I always had a better day when I started my day this way. My last hour consisted of journaling, reflecting and reading a paper book. I'd dim the lights and quieted my space with either meditative music or silence. No phone/iPad in bed. Staying away from screens before bed is tough but so important for overall health. You'll sleep better and that's just what tomorrow needs.

REboot Express: Do Hard Things With Courage

When things got down to the nitty gritty and I knew only big moves were coming next, I had a serious talk with myself. If I was going to change my life and move beyond the pain I was in, I had to make bold moves within. I also knew I needed a huge supply of courage. Creating a daily discipline of mind, body and soul activities seemed like the most logical thing to do. I created and committed to a six week boot camp for myself. I figured it works for the military, it should work for me. I decided that if I could follow through with a six week commitment, I would be strong enough to face the difficult things in front of me. This was the single biggest factor in getting me through the unmarrying process. A daily discipline of strengthening my mind, body and soul created the indomitable emotional spirit and courage I needed to make the leaps I needed to make.

I committed to a combination of adding and losing habits as well as creating comforting rituals and routines. All things together grew a strength inside of me that could never be found by just reading a book or heeding advice. It's the inside work that ultimately creates the major life change you seek.

My boot camp was life changing and I continue to re-enlist in it to this day to help me continue to thrive. Now I'm so excited to say that I've perfected the process and created tools to help others conquer major life changes gracefully as well. To learn more and join me, go to SomethingJustClicked.co m. I'm so excited to share my REboot Express with you!

About the Author

Maria Valentine

Maria never considered herself a writer, even though she always has been. As an entrepreneur who wears many hats, her journalism degree has been put to good use in the span of her career. As a homeschooling mom, she even published a magazine written entirely by kids, guiding and inspiring hundreds of kids all over the world to write. But that doesn't mean she considered herself a writer.

It hadn't been until she wrote *UnMarrying My Best Friend* that Maria embraced the idea that writing was more than just something she did a lot.

Take the millions of words she's strung together in articles, journals, websites and more, and yes a writer she is.

But now a book? An author she be.

Post divorce, Maria is coming into a new world of her own making with a new name and new life. Every day she strives to lead from love while keeping an eye on her inner gremlin.

Get to know Maria more and keep up with her new books and programs at SomethingJustClicked.com. And Instagram @somethingjustclicked.

Made in the USA
Columbia, SC
16 January 2025

51977414R00098